Glorious Food
Catherine von Ruhland was born in North West London and currently lives in a crumbling old vicarage behind a church in West Hounslow. She has a degree in librarianship from Manchester Polytechnic, but has never worked as a librarian. Now in publishing, she has previously worked as a journalist for a number of papers, was employed by Tear Fund in their Editorial Department and was Publications Editor at the Evangelical Alliance. She is the author of *Going Green*.

*Books available from Marshall Pickering
by the same author*

Going Green – a Christian guide

Glorious Food

From Fasting to Feasting – a Christian guide

by
Catherine von Ruhland

Marshall Pickering
An Imprint of HarperCollins*Publishers*

Marshall Pickering is an Imprint of
HarperCollins*Religious*
Part of HarperCollins*Publishers*
77–85 Fulham Palace Road, London W6 8JB

First published in Great Britain
in 1992 by Marshall Pickering

1 3 5 7 9 10 8 6 4 2

A catalogue record for this book is
available from the British Library

ISBN 0 551 02374–0

Phototypeset by Intype Ltd, London
Printed and bound in Great Britain by
HarperCollinsManufacturing Glasgow

To Claire, Frances, Naomi, Jane,
Juliet, Pauline and Sally.
Friends for life. May we be
friends for ever.

Contents

1
Introduction

Is God really interested in what I had for breakfast this morning? When I'm in my local newsagent's trying to choose between forking out for a Yorkie or a tube of Smarties, should I ask His advice? Is it OK to be overweight or obsessed with diets *and* a friend of Jesus?

Like sleep, a supply of oxygen and water, food is a basic necessity. But the rich variety of flavourings, tastes, colours and texture reveal something of God's wondrous creativity and the goodness of His gifts. Yet for many, food represents a life of tyranny, an uncontrollable obsession or plain old poison for others. Not to mention those who simply don't have enough. Somewhere along the line we seem to have forgotten to look out for the mark of our Creator on the food we eat.

For when Jesus declared to the Devil that man cannot live by bread alone,[1] He emphasized the importance of spiritual sustenance too. If we are to eat properly, in the true sense of the word, then we must put the food on our plates and the drink we drink under the microscope of our Christian faith.

Then we begin to understand its role in a more complete way. The general trend may be towards pre-packed meals, vitamin pills and microwave cooking, with the intention of making meals last as short a time as possible. We may worry about additives, food surpluses and shortages and the treatment of livestock. But God turns things round, puts things in perspective and shows us that eating is also a time to enjoy His rich provision in itself.

That's not to say that we ignore the downside of the food industry. In fact, by celebrating the feast in a Christian context we actually have our eyes opened to the social and political impact of our eating patterns. We stop to think about our food.

We're rightly concerned about the amount of additives that have been added to our diets, how food is over-refined, and the scares that surround our farm animals, but we should be aware that apparently healthy alternatives aren't always what they seem.

Take a look around your local health food store. Mine now has weights in the window and one side of the shop devoted to pills and potions. My aunt, a doctor, tells me that on popping into such a shop for a snack bar on one occasion, she was horrified by the range of supplements and medicines on display. 'What sort of health is this?', she asked herself. For, let's face it, if health food stores were *really* into promoting health, they'd be advocating a balanced diet rather than regular pill-popping.

Some people argue that you need to take vitamin supplements these days just because you can't be sure that your food contains all the nutrients you need for good health. I'd argue that you'd be better off checking what you *do* eat and altering your diet accordingly. If you're not sure if you get enough vitamin C, for example, don't reach for the pill box. Have an orange instead.

It's as simple as that. The healthiest I ever felt was the time when as a student I decided to opt for a vegetarian wholefood diet. I have a big appetite, but I didn't need to scrimp on my food. I simply made sure that anything I did eat was unrefined. If I made a cake or pudding I used natural ingredients, honey or raw sugar instead of refined alternatives. Combined with cycling eight miles a day to and from college I managed to lose a stone in a month without even thinking about it, and I felt truly alert. If I'd had the business acumen of Rosemary 'Hip and Thigh' Conley I could have made a fortune.

Of course, all of the meals I made had that uniform brown hue that so much health food has. But returning to a hall of residence after my year of living healthily I was repelled by the processed food that was on offer. So used to the earthy brown of my flour, bread and buns; the stark white of the sliced bread and sugar on my morning bowl of cornflakes looked obscene. Any goodness that the food had once contained had so obviously been bleached out of it. I must admit, I've never quite understood why if there's ever a bread shortage, people don't stop to think about the utter absurdity of this and so consider alternatives. They queue for low quality, 'plastic' bread when they could make their own far healthier loaves at a fraction of the cost.

God has provided the food for us. Certainly a lot needs work on it before we can eat it, but that doesn't mean that it has to be processed beyond recognition. So much food is just waiting to be harvested. But in its distribution and sale, the bottom line is that without the refining process there isn't much money to be made. 'Generally speaking, it is not whole, fresh food, but highly processed food with its "added value" that makes the money. From the business point of view, a potato is small potatoes. Better, is a chip. Better still is a crisp. Best of all, is a crunchy waffle.'[2]

Which literally goes against the grain. There's so much natural, God-given goodness to be found in food that's never seen a factory conveyor belt or supermarket shelf. And when we eat food from which that goodness has been extracted, our health suffers. In her fascinating study *Fruits of the earth*,[3] Anne Arnott not only reveals the delicious and nutritional treasures that God has made available to help us live, but the utter joy of seeing her young son crushing his glasses underfoot after his shortsightedness had been cured by feeding him vitamin B-rich homemade wholewheat bread.

It's well-known that many 'old wives tales' harbour a lot of truth. And that herbs, for example, as well as making a fine cup of tea or adding subtle flavours to soups, can also be used for medicinal purposes. That's got nothing to do with any conjuring of spells or New Age influence. Whenever I have a cold I'll just as readily concoct a soothing hot honey and lemon drink as knock back the Galloways cough mixture. A teaspoonful of honey with a squirt of lemon juice in a mug of hot water makes a naturally healthy but harmless recipe.

When Paul declared in his letter to the Corinthians that our bodies are the temple of the Holy Spirit,[4] it was as advice to treat our bodies with respect. 'God has chosen to dwell in the physical body of those who believe in Him. So my body has a very important function. It is a residence of the Holy Spirit and I believe that it is pleasing to God that I keep that residence of the Holy Spirit in the best possible condition. It should be healthy and strong and able to do the things God wants done.'[5]

But while we'll happily have a good discussion about an issue that's provoking us, or try to listen to what the Holy Spirit is saying, it's rare that we'll take the trouble to listen to what God is telling us through our physical nature. Sure, we respond to external stimuli through touch or things which cause pain, for example, but what of our own physical still, small voice within us which doesn't stop at pain, hunger or thirst? We listen to our thoughts. We should listen to our bodies too when they get cravings or seem over-tired.

For in the same way that we might suddenly and inexplicably find the name of the friend flash across our mind as God nudges us to get in touch with them, maybe because they need our support, so our body talks to us, telling us what we should be feeding it. We've all heard of women who've had cravings for such things as oranges (vitamin C) and even chalk (calcium) during their pregnancies.

During my childhood I was forever needing a drink. We'd be on a family holiday walking out in the middle of nowhere and I'd plaintively pipe up, 'Mum, I'm thirsty'. I still vividly recall queueing up with all the other primary school kids for a slug from the drinking fountain one hot summer's day, and being thrown out of the washroom without any water by an angry dinner lady because I was impatient enough to call out to the child at the head of the queue to hurry up! As it happened, years later it turned out that I'd had kidney disease since birth; a seemingly insatiable thirst is a classic symptom.

Maybe you've wondered why so many adverts for chocolate bars and drinks feature professional looking women guzzling the stuff in solitary splendour, whether it's Josie Lawrence with her 'moon-chees' stretched out on a chaise-longue or a sharp-suited business woman curled in hiding under her desk while she pigs out on a walnut whip. It's because an awful lot of women have been there.

For a lot of us, being a bit down on a monthly basis is a good excuse to bite into a Bitz bar to cheer ourselves up. But, in fact, it's not actually an excuse. Your body simply tells you it wants chocolate. Me, I'm not the argumentative type.

It's an accepted fact that chocolate contains phenylethylane, a chemical which is very similar to that which your body produces when you're in love. So the inverse is that if you're not too happy with life, you want to get that good feeling back. Mind you, I've discovered that munching a Yorkie in a room on your own to the strains of Tracy Chapman's song 'Fast Car' (not at the time being in the mood for anything more cheery) has the opposite effect. . . .

A young woman I once worked with told me how having broken up with her boyfriend, she was visited one evening by close friends who wanted to console her. She suddenly declared to everyone that she was going to the off-licence. None of her friends said a word, but she recalled that they all looked darkly at each other and she could see them all thinking, 'Uh, oh, she's going on a bender'. Ten minutes later she was back laden down with choc bars and bags of sweets. She sat in the middle of the floor with a massive pile of confectionary in front of her and wolfed the lot!

Cravings can easily get out of hand, but so can the guilt and ill-feeling that often follow. Women in particular are conditioned to regard sugary, high calorie foods as strictly off-limits. The images they see around them in magazines, films and clothes shops in the high street are of sylph-like beauties. They are taught from an early age that that is how a woman is meant to look, and that they'll never catch a man if they don't look the part. Instead of being a pleasurable experience as God surely meant it to be, the very act of eating is transformed into a painful tyranny.

But keeping close to God helps us break those myths, though for the anorexic or indeed anyone obsessed by diet it can be a long slow process.

When we look at our food in the light of our faith we find that we see food for what it is. God gives us wisdom by helping us see things with His eyes. Years ago when caffeine-free coffee was still very new, I visited some Christian friends who declared that they didn't drink ordinary coffee any more because of its drug content. At the time it struck me as a bit over the top, but months later it suddenly clicked for me too. I understood that if you regard your body as God's temple, then you don't want to be feeding it with poisonous substances. And thinking like that actually helps us to give them up more easily.

For though as Christians our whole daily lives should glorify God; through the choices we make, what we say, our activities, and, yes, our meals and the choices we make about the food we eat; that's easier said than done. It's so easy to become complacent. Certainly we should be thankful for everything God has given us. It should go without saying. But because we are only human, we can tend to forget this. For that reason, saying Grace before a meal, a quick 'Thanks, God' before we bite into a snack, is a way of getting us into the right frame of mind.

Even just a simple 'for what we are about to receive . . .', if we think about what we're actually saying, helps transform the means to satisfy a basic bodily need into something holy. We literally see our food in a new light. I find that after a spate of cooking and when I've set out my meal on the table, saying Grace helps me pause for breath and appreciate all the different stages from the planting

of the seed to the final dish. I also find it much
easier to say Grace when I've been part of the
production process as opposed to getting my food
out of a packet.

Admittedly Grace said at certain times and
places can come across as not much more than a
religious tradition. Schoolchildren daily chant the
lunchtime prayer without much thought, and I've
been at dinners where Grace was recited in Latin!
Since the height of my Latin education was playing
the part of the wall ('Ego sum murus . . .') in a
stage play of Pyramus and Thisbe, I'm afraid Latin
Grace is beyond me. The experience was similar
to when I attended a Norwegian service in an Oslo
church. I knew that something spiritual was being
said, didn't have much of a clue what, but feebly
hoped that I could offer it to God anyway. As for
my own personal spiritual satisfaction, I can't say
either experience was of much help.

But bringing a spiritual approach to our food
certainly is. After all, it was precisely because Eve
ignored the vital ingredient of spiritual truth –
God's loving command not to eat the fruit from
the tree that stood in the middle of the Garden of
Eden – that the world's in the mess it is. She
succumbed to the temptation of self-satisfaction,
and with her husband poisoned all our souls.

'When the woman saw that the fruit of the tree
was good for food and pleasing to the eye, and
also desirable for gaining wisdom, she took some
and ate it. She also gave some to her husband who
was with her, and he ate it. Then the eyes of both

of them were opened, and they realized that they were naked.'[6]

It's our self-satisfaction, our sinfulness that causes all the problems. We ignore how our eating habits force people in the Third World to exist on starvation diets, gorge ourselves on burgers, cream cakes and sweets, and we refuse to take account of the suffering of God's creatures in order that we can get meat on our plates. If we only gave God a thought when we took a bite we'd be far less likely to allow our own desire to direct our choice of food.

Though to my knowledge not Christians, Linda and Paul McCartney have revealed that it was while delighting in the frolicking of the lambs on their farm, seen from their window whilst eating their home-grown dinner, that they were brought to their senses. They looked down at what they were eating, looked at each other and realized what was lying on their plates. They'd made the connection.

Few of us have such a dramatic opportunity to come face-to-face with the direct consequences of our eating patterns, but God does make us receptive to the truth, and as Christians it's up to us to make a point of finding out. It's not enough to be *concerned* about factory farming, food mountains, the starving in the Third *and* First World, food additives and pesticides. We can actually *do* something. That may mean eating foodstuffs that lessen our impact on God's creation, or campaigning in other ways – for example by writing to our MP, or supporting a Third World development agency.

It's about bringing a Christian perspective to the whole issue of food. And because it's a Christian perspective it's about celebrating the feast. It's a celebration of the hope we have in Christ Jesus.

The very art of sitting down at a table together is quite something, yet how many of us do that these days? The whole way of selling food is eroding that basic activity. Somebody once said that poverty is not being able to eat together. In a spiritual sense, there's a lot of truth in that. There's something about sitting together to relate as a family or household and retelling the day's happenings to each other at the end of a day. And it's certainly very important when it comes to children's mental and social growth and their development as a human to be able to relate stories and shared experiences. Tony Campolo reveals how uniting in such a way has benefited his own family in his joyful book *The Kingdom of God is a Party*. 'In my own family, each of us had an obligation to share something "funny" that had happened during the day. It was no wonder that all of the Campolos became incredible storytellers. When our family got together at meal times we all knew we were in for a good time. Meal time was party time at our house.'[7]

The breaking down of the family, whether that's through the divorce courts or just by accepting what we've been sold – those TV dinners, microwave ovens and take-aways – leads ultimately to a breakdown in society. From pot noodles to anarchy? That seems quite a strange connection to make, but by regarding food as simply a commodity, a necessary inconvenience to our work schedule (remember Michael Douglas in the movie *Wall Street* declaring that 'lunch is for wimps'?), or leisure hours, the food manufacturers are steadily eroding the art of eating together and the human ties that are strengthened through that experience. At Christmas time you can now buy individual portions of Christmas pudding. Not only is that terribly sad, but it represents the dangerous state of individualism that our society has reached: that when it comes to food it's everyone for themselves.

Remember all those old sci-fi movies, when a delicious three-course meal comes in the form of a tiny capsule you swallow? No doubt a lot of housewives feel that that might as well be the case, after the meal they've spent hours preparing is guzzled down by gannets in a matter of moments. Yet people who are so keen not to make a meal of their food are missing out on what a meal is in itself.

Maybe you no longer live with your immediate family. Perhaps you rent a house with others or live on your own. There's no need to stop partying! My closest friends I've known since I was at least eleven or twelve. Because we all went to the same secondary school we have a common history. Though geographically we are beginning to go our separate ways and we work in different professions and lead our own separate lives, when we meet over dinner for a 'girls' night in' at someone's home we have a real laugh. We crack up about what we got up to during our school days yet continue our story together through such meetings. The husbands and boyfriends are left at home for the evening or make a quick exit, and we're left to reminisce over a meal, and then perhaps watch a video or just natter the night away. In such a situation, the food almost becomes secondary yet paradoxically retains a real importance. The cooking, the preparation and the giving of oneself in the process as well as the food itself are lifted up to God simply *because* it's all brought people together. And the meal doesn't have to be anything grand. It can be as basic as a huge bowl of pasta, plenty of salad, and yoghurt and fresh fruit to follow.

Again and again in the gospels we see Jesus and His disciples eating together, sharing food, feeding the five thousand, and ultimately around the table at what has become known as the Last Supper. With a number of them being fishermen by profession they also knew a lot about what they were eating; they'd pulled it out of the sea with their own hands. They knew the laws of the sea and the weather; the tides, the colour of the skies and their environment. Eating fish together was a natural extension of this lifestyle, it was part of their personal landscapes. They were fisherman who ate fish and to whom Jesus said 'I will make you fishers of men'.[8] Jesus was adept at speaking great truths in a language that His listeners understood: 'Once again, the kingdom of heaven is like a net that was let down into the lake and caught all kinds of fish. When it was full, the fishermen pulled it up on the shore. Then they sat down and collected the good fish in baskets, but threw the bad away.'[9] The imagery rang very deep.

These days, because of our modern lifestyles, we're far away from our food. Christian Grace, and indeed our Christian faith, *does* pull us up short. Like any prayer, it helps us to stop and think, and that's a very important part of our Christian life. And if we do put food in its proper context we've also got to take into account all the negative things connected with food. During my research for this book, I happened to mention to a guy I was interviewing about his experience of anorexia that I was thinking of calling this book 'Glorious Food'. He grimaced a bit – which I can quite understand – simply because his own experience with food was of purging and near-starvation. Other people are starving just because they haven't got enough to eat; they're just too poor. Added to that there's all the additives and such like. We need to remember that food made from natural ingredients is food provided by God. Food in its proper place is food given to God and honoured by Him too. It's transformed. As Christians it's up to us to make sure Jesus is a guest at every meal.

2
Mirror, Mirror on the Wall

The choice we make about what we fill our stomachs with is very much tied to our own self-image, of who we are as a person. People who don't have a high regard for themselves, who see themselves as not worth the effort, can veer towards obesity, while anorexia can be the last resort of those who, under authority or feeling the ultimate victim of circumstance, have no other way of asserting themselves.

It's certainly very easy to point the finger, particularly at people who appear overweight, and declare that their obesity is sinful, as some are wont to do. Yet it could be argued that the amount of money spent on slimming products and invested in the slimming industry is just as bad, and that the message expressed by our society that to be slim is to be beautiful/glamorous/successful is one of the worst tyrannies bestowed on many women *and* men.

From an early age children learn that being overweight isn't attractive. They're ridiculed in sports lessons, the butt of classroom jokes. But for girls in particular it is especially hurtful. Such abuse strikes at their very identity within society, and unnerves a potentially fragile sense of self: 'There is a crucial moment in the life of a little girl, a decisive ordeal after which nothing is as it was before. Watch them jostle at the school gate. It takes no more than a glance to recognize the innocent ones, the ones who have not yet undergone the ordeal. They may be skinny or plump, graceful or gauche, radiant or melancholy, but it is obvious that it doesn't bother them, they aren't even aware of it. The others, the ones who have been through the ordeal, the initiates, recognize themselves in the mirror they carry deep in their hearts. One accursed day, these girls have asked themselves the question (fateful, yet so absurd): "Am I pretty?" What happens at that moment is that the whole alienation of the feminine condition falls on their shoulders. Yes, women ought to militate to be granted, as men are, the right to be ugly.'[1]

It doesn't get any easier as a girl gets older. Comics and the glossy magazines insist that she keep her weight down (while incongruously providing her with recipes for mouth-watering, calorie-filled cakes). After all, it's implied, a man will only love her if she makes sure she looks good for him (it also being implied that her life's aim must be to find a man . . .). It doesn't help that when young girls reach puberty, their metabolism slows down and they begin to build up reserves of fat, so that where once they could compete with their brothers in the pig-out stakes without necessarily putting on weight, they're suddenly pulled up short. As their bodies evolve into more womanly figures, they realize, too, the potential they have to lose their shape completely if they eat as much as they did before.

Male or female, we should all to a certain extent keep our weight in check. Certainly there is something to be said for getting rid of the excess. Being overweight simply isn't good for your health. In traditional societies, such as in Africa, heart disease was until recently virtually unknown. But the growing consumption of Western foods which are high in fat and sugar has made heart disease a new problem in the Third World, one that never existed before. In our society it is rife.

But taking care of ourselves through the choices we make about what we eat doesn't mean getting obsessed with dieting, but eating sensibly so that we keep the shape God wants us to be.

It means making sure our bodies are well-toned, but at the same time being happy with our individual shape, whether that's large or small, ectomorph or endomorph (that is, long and thin or more rounded). There's a famous prayer that Sinead O'Connor recites at the beginning of her album 'I do not want what I haven't got': 'Lord, give me the serenity to accept the things I cannot change, the courage to change the things I can, and the wisdom to know the difference.' It would be wise if we all bore this in mind when it came to the way we looked.

For with that in mind we can learn to accept ourselves, knowing that regardless of our shape and looks God values us and regards us as part of His beautiful creation. Perhaps one of the more dreadful legacies of the Fall is that our Godly view of things became tarnished. It is said that beauty is in the eye of the beholder. Whereas God looked on everything and saw that it was good,[2] our darkened perceptions interpret God's created beauty in a negative light. As Adam and Eve realized they were naked once they had eaten the forbidden fruit,[3] so we perceive things *and* people as 'ugly'. It is only love that shields our eyes from seeing this way.

Otherwise we are sucked into the worldly myth that physical 'beauty' (whatever that means) is far more important than the person who happens to reside in the body, and not only that, but in this society womanly perfection is a size ten (preferably eight) figure combined with a limited supply of brain cells; otherwise known as the 'bimbo'. Which ignores the fact that we are all valuable *and* beautiful in God's sight, whatever our size or shape (or brain power, come to that). 'When vulnerable ten-year-olds are increasingly being drawn into the dreadful, self-destructive cycle of binge/purge/ starvation, surely we should consider why we are defending a whole culture based on such an extremely narrow view of female worth.'[4]

It can be just as tough for men. Poor Paul Gasgoigne had to suffer the indignity (and the pain) of having Mars Bars rain down on him from the terraces while he battled to keep his weight down. Early on in his career Cliff Richard, who was beginning to lose the hungry, smouldering look he'd started out with because he was now able to afford decent meals, was humiliated in front of millions of TV viewers when Coronation Street's Minnie Caldwell declared, 'I do love that chubby Cliff Richard' on screen. (I'll wager it was at that moment that he lost his street cred!) He now looks very good on one meal a day and the odd dose of vitamin pills, ginseng and royal jelly. Men probably put on weight just as easily as women, but it's more acceptable for the male to look stocky, just as it is for them to look their age.

The healthy self-image we *should* carry inside our heads is very close to the person God sees. Admittedly, for so many people their own self-image tends to be distorted. As even Dame Judi Dench admits: 'I've got these very long, long legs, and I'm blond, a slim blonde, then suddenly I catch sight of myself in the mirror and I'm horrified. We are all conditioned to do this because of those magazines, looking at those sickening girls.'[5]

In fact, it's our *mirror* image that we need to come to terms with, for that is the most regular image of ourselves we are ever likely to see. One wonders about the people who have existed without photos or mirrors; is their self-image much less fragile? Or conversely, even more so, being perhaps based solely on how *others* perceive them?

In this society our dissatisfaction with the way we look lies in the fact that very few of us, even the models themselves, live up to the media image of humankind, and partly because we are just not used to seeing the view of us that others see. The only place we can feel ourself in this sense is when we come face-to-face in the mirror. It's probably one of the best places to begin the journey to accepting oneself. After all, God does. Take a good look at your reflection and tell yourself 'God loves me'. In a sense, it doesn't matter what you or others think of the way you look. It's how God sees you that matters. He, as we all know, is most interested in the person within.

Fat lot of good?

Nevertheless, people who appear overweight are at a distinct disadvantage. In the same way that well-fed dieticians are not a good advert for their work, so it is a bit difficult for bulky Christians to talk about their concern for the starving of the world; they just don't look the part. We've all heard of the Western development agencies that provide banquets at their meetings. It doesn't impress. In the same way, by the way we look, we are giving a message that appears hypocritical even though it's probably not the whole story.

Not only that, but this is one symptom of a much greater world sickness. While in the Third World young children are lucky to reach their fifth birthday, and malnutrition, if not starvation itself, is rife, in the Western world we are dying of excess. Perhaps if anything this shows in grisly black and white the real inequalities of our world, which hit us right between the teeth.

Mind you, I'm always wary of people who bluntly declare that *all* fat people are fat because they eat too much. Others will go so far as to say that

being fat is a sin for the very same reason. Which-
ever, it is generally put across with a distinct lack
of compassion.

As they get older, many people do balloon out
a bit. Maybe it's the hormones or their metabolism
slowing down. Or maybe they do overeat. We
should give them the benefit of the doubt, simply
because we don't know the reason why someone
appears overweight. Maybe they eat for comfort,
or poor diet has taken its toll on their physique;
and it doesn't necessarily leave people skinny.
More often than not it results in a sickly pallor,
mental sluggishness, unhealthy skin (calling a zit-
ridden mate 'pizza face' may be closer to the mark
than you realize!) and a stodgy look that reflects
the carbohydrates and junk food that people are
encouraged to live on. Despite efforts by the fast
food chains, for instance, to persuade consumers
that their food is nutritionally sound, it is generally
accepted in medical circles that it is in fact low in
food value.

Hanging out at my local Burger King I find it
fascinating to people-watch. Where twenty years
ago there were still kids around who looked fairly
scrawny, now many have what I find myself calling the 'burger kid' look. I recognize it from images
I've seen of American children; that tubby round
look that doesn't bode well for the child's future
health. Indeed, compared with 1946, twice as
many British children are now obese and have
eczema, six times as many have diabetes and three
times as many have asthma! But then, in 1946
the nation's diet had improved dramatically simply

because of rationing. Poor families who previously simply went without the food they could not afford, now had access to a well-balanced diet. How many children today are fed so well?

Still, I'm one to talk. Having been on steroid drugs for half of my life I've developed the stubby figure and 'moon' face that are classic side effects. I recall when as a teenager I'd have my regular check-ups at the renal clinic. It was like walking onto the set of some surreal version of John Wyndham's book *The Midwich Cuckoos*. All the children had this moonface look; it was like a David Lynch remake of *Village of the Damned*. It doesn't help that the drugs also give you a vast appetite, and that any weight you do put on goes directly onto your face. It's rare that my square jawline gets a look-in, and my poor little button nose can look quite lost!

When anybody has callously made a remark about my shape, I've just put it down to ignorance. We should be very careful what we say about each other. A number of the female anorexics I spoke to when researching this book told me that it was a chance remark by a boyfriend about their weight that had set them off on the road to ruin. And that saying 'You look good' to an anorexic will be interpreted as 'You look fat', or to say that they look skinny is to say that they look slim which they'll feel pleased about. . . .

It's very easy to gain a wrong impression of yourself from how others perceive you. As a child, not only did my dear bro Chris disown me when I started at Infants School the year after he did

('She's not my sister'!), but for years he delighted in calling me 'Fatty'. Thinking about it now makes me laugh, for if anything he was the one with the appetite. My mum's friend Grace said of the boy as she watched him wolf down his food that it was like giving strawberries to donkeys! My mother used to give us nicknames from the list of Dr Seuss books on the back of the *Cat in the Hat* books we brought home from primary school. I can't remember my nickname, but Jane was 'No Funny Business' because she had quite a mischievous streak. And Chris was 'Last One Home's A Green Pig' because he ate so much! Yet I look at the photos from our childhood and in fact none of us were overweight, though I had been a big baby.

Since each one of us has to look at our own face and body every morning, and God as our Creator happened to make that piece of humanity, and presumably *He* likes it, then we've surely every right to regard ourselves as OK to look at, whatever the world might call us. Women like Roseanne Barr and Claudia 'Blind Date' Patrice are challenging what is essentially a Hollywood image of women. In other cultures, being well-rounded is openingly regarded as very attractive; Claudia admits to having had men throw roses at her when she walked down the street in Italy. Those Latino boys called her a goddess too. . . . In the same way that followers of Christ can call themselves princes or princesses, as God's children we *know* that we are beautiful.

Slim chance

The pressure on women to look slim has reached a dangerous level. Younger and younger girls are caught up in the diet trap as their older sisters and mothers were before them. Theirs will be a lifetime spent worrying about their weight while neglecting the pleasures of God's provision. There's something very sad about hearing a child of junior school age decline a piece of food because 'it's fattening'. Where's their *joie de vivre*? Where's their childhood? Now, if a child has been brought up on a balanced diet, then the odd bit of party fare is hardly going to make a great deal of difference to their health.

There seems to be something in women in particular that is never satisfied. We feel that we could always be a shade more slim. But bodily perfection is an unattainable goal. After all, think of all those women who'd love to look like Julia Roberts in *Pretty Woman*, and then learn that it apparently wasn't her body that was filmed most of the time. Doesn't that say it all; that the stunning Julia Roberts wasn't happy wearing hot pants? There's irony too in the fact that those who are perceived through Hollywood's eyes to be some of the world's most beautiful women are the ones most likely to have had, and to have, an assortment of nips and tucks, nose jobs and silicon implants.

There's a lot of pressure on men too. Whenever I see teenage lads buying that quick weight-building powder you add to drinks, at my local health food store, it makes me sad. It's almost as if woman's general obsession with her looks is spreading into the male world too. It's as if to get the girl they have to look the part. I have a theory that some men who feel threatened by the more assertive women of this age feel that they've got to emphasize their masculinity, develop their machismo, to show who they think is boss.

It's healthy for neither men nor women. Top model Yasmin le Bon suffered a number of miscarriages before she and Duranie husband Simon had a little girl – which may or may not have been connected with the strict regime of an international model. Many of today's models look seriously undernourished. (That other type of model, the euphemistically named 'glamour' girl of page three and her more developed sisters who line the top shelf of the local newsagents, just look deformed.) If you ever see the movie *Scandal* about the 1960s Profumo affair, consider that 1980s actresses Bridget Fonda and Joanne Whalley-Kilmer who portrayed Mandy Rice Davis and Christine Keeler looked at least a couple of clothes sizes skinnier than the real and much younger women. Yet Christine and Mandy were very much the shape of their day. Today's models are very angular and androgynous; many have lost the rounded curves of womanhood.

As Christians we should be happy with our bodies. Knowing that God loves us, we learn to love ourselves. Which should make it easier for us to keep in trim, for we have all the right motivation for keeping fit and healthy. Which, admittedly, is easier said than done.

What was so good about Rosemary Conley's oh-so-successful Hip and Thigh diet was that in itself it wasn't so much of a diet (in the conventional sense), as a guide to eating sensibly and healthily that trimmed people too. Herself a Christian, she was very clever in marketing what was basically a medical health food diet and turning it into a best-seller for all types of women. And what's more, for them it actually works. She also avoided the obsession with counting calories. After all, who needs them?

Yet so many women are caught in the diet trap. Indeed, a Gallup poll commissioned by *New Woman* magazine discovered that eighty-nine per cent of women want to change their weight, but only five per cent want to increase it. And forty-two per cent think that their bodies are wrongly proportioned.[6] From cutting down on their food intake, they can so easily become dangerously obsessed with their image to a distorting degree. In fact, one fifteen-year-old in every 150 suffers from an eating disorder.

Anorexia nervosa is a dieting addiction that has people literally starving themselves in an attempt to keep their weight down. Skeletally thin, she (and most cases of anorexia occur among young women) still sees herself as fat. Ironically, the anorexic often feels that dieting is the one way she can be in control of her life; often their lives are dreadfully stressful, but in reality, anorexia is the ultimate loss of self-control; it is dieting to death.

There's often a lot of deceit involved too; a denial to friends and self that anything is wrong, and a deceiving way of skipping meals.

Bulimia nervosa is a similar eating disorder. Yet where the anorexic avoids food, the bulimic often diets savagely until in a fit of hunger and sheer unhappiness she binges on whatever food is to hand. Interestingly enough, Rosemary Conley identifies bingeing as a direct result of strict dieting, and in particular of calorie counting: 'We are able to cope with a restricted diet for most of the day, but four o'clock arrives, we've munched our way through most of our daily allowance and the prospect of a slim-line evening is just too much. We nibble a little to start with, then it turns into a wholesale binge. We throw in the towel and say, "Oh well, I'll start properly tomorrow".'[7]

It is not unknown for a bulimic to wolf her way through the entire food contents of the kitchen. And then she feels utter remorse and disgust at what she had done and makes herself sick.

As with any addiction, it is by admitting to yourself and friends and family that you have a problem that you can begin to work your way out of the deep pit. As a Christian that means admitting it to God too. If you are afraid that someone you know has an eating disorder, develop their trust and confidence so that they feel free to disclose what they are going through. Over the next few pages, five Christians, themselves victims of eating disorders, disclose their experiences. I have altered their names to preserve anonymity, but I have done nothing to their stories. I make no comment on what they say, but give them the space to explain themselves. Consider and try to understand their experiences, and use the information they provide to help you respond to people you know with eating disorders. Maybe you share their experience. Take anything from what they say that will help you find the way out; may God work through these pages for you.

RUTH is an attractive young woman. A slightly shy seventeen-year-old, there's little indication of the hell she experienced when she decided to lose a bit of weight to attract the eye of a guy she really liked. Dieting took over: 'I lost two stone, my periods stopped and during a spate of dizzy spells I ended up in hospital.

'It did strange things to my head. I couldn't enjoy myself at any social event where there wasn't any food, but if food was there, I couldn't eat it. I just couldn't understand how people could enjoy themselves without having food around. At the time I was organizing my local Scripture Union group socials. After six barbeques in a row, people got rather fed up', she laughs. 'I felt that that was what people would enjoy doing most; eating!

'I suppose there is something in the way women appear in magazines and films. I knew that if you're slim, you're considered to be good looking, that slim equals beautiful. Originally I was just over ten stone. By the time I'd finished dieting I'd lost two stone, which in a sense isn't much, but it was enough to upset my body metabolism.

Though I've been up to my normal weight for a year, I still get panicky if I've eaten during the day and then go out for a meal in the evening', she admits. 'When I was really ill I couldn't control what I was eating. I knew I was against it, but somehow my hand got into the bread bin or biscuit tin.

'My family completely ignored my ordeal', Ruth discloses. 'My mum refused to believe it even when I was hospitalized. My friends tried to warn me, but I said "Not me, not likely". I'd be thinking "Oh, yeah, that'd be good". In a way I suppose I was seeking attention', she admits. 'In fact, I didn't see that guy for another year!' she smiles. 'It got to really irk me that mum wasn't noticing, that it had to get to the point of me going to hospital when I was dying.'

It was GCSEs that pulled Ruth out of her anorexic state, but she doesn't feel completely cured. 'I had so much time for revising that I ended up bingeing and putting on a stone in weight. That terrified me. I thought I'd turn out to be the biggest person in the world', she recalls. 'I'll still look at a friend who I know is a size fourteen, and I'm a size twelve, and think that they're thinner than me. I *know* they're obviously not, but it's a gut reaction. The whole thing is really strange because you don't feel that you're you.

'When I was in hospital, they didn't really do a great deal except send me back to my GP, who told me that the whole thing was "just my age". I don't completely know when I started to pull out of it. I didn't go from eating very little to eating

normally, I went through a stage of eating everything in sight. I still feel guilty about eating.
Basically the whole thing is an obsession with food
and a denial of that at the same time, and then
from that to an obsession without the denial. . . .

'The most supportive people were my church
fellowship who were praying with me, and my
Scripture Union group. They'd realized something
was wrong. One of the staff leaders had a little
boy, and I happened to comment that the child
was too fat. The leader was shocked: "Ruth, is
that all you think about, being fat and food?" But
during that time I'd completely backslidden. My
food obsession was completely at the centre of my
life. Since then I don't feel as close to God as I did
before. I used to chat away to Him on the way to
school, but that doesn't happen any more. I don't
think I'd have got through it if I wasn't a Christian,
though. Somehow God stopped me from making
myself sick. If I'd started doing that it would have
been far more dangerous. I did pray about what I
was going through, but when it came to "Thy will
be done" I knew that if it was God's will that I put
weight back on, I didn't want to know.'

Ruth looks back on her dieting phase, which got
out of hand, as a completely pointless exercise.
'The only thing I did was spend a lot of money on
a smaller wardrobe that has since been packed off
to charity shops! It also made me more aware that
I can't be condemning of people, because sometimes you get into a hole you can't get out of. We
all keep doing the same things over and over
again. People are addicted to drugs and alcohol,

which is really just the same as over-eating, yet while Christians were always very loving and understanding towards me, I find it hard to understand why people seem to grade sins. Pigging out and making yourself sick when people are starving is far more acceptable than committing adultery over and over again, yet they're both physical acts.'

SHEILA, also in her late teens, suffers from bulimia, which began to emerge when she went away to boarding school for her last year. 'It developed from the beginning of term; because I was new there, I felt isolated. I'm sure others at school knew I was making myself sick, but they never said anything. Now I've a friend at college in whom I've confided and she's very supportive.

'The problem was that I thought I was worthless. I still hate looking at myself in the mirror, and I hate the way I feel', she admits. 'I'm trying to grab all the love I can get; I've been really testing my boyfriend that way. So often I think I'm cured, but the whole thing is a vicious circle. I can see that what I'm doing is damaging, yet when I have any problems I find I want to eat and eat to block it all out. I do have warning bells, but I completely ignore them until they disappear, and then I realize, "Oh no, I've done it again". At those times I'll eat anything I know is bad for me and which I wouldn't normally eat. At other times I'll be able to fast for a whole day. Sometimes I have even wished that I was anorexic, to stop myself eating.

'My boyfriend and mother just don't understand; they think it's simply all in the mind and easy to stop. I really long for support from them. You can usually tell if people are lying about what they're eating, particularly if they've got a major problem or difficulty that's playing on their mind that doesn't seem to be affecting them. Friends and families should watch out for that', she advises.

'If I can offer any advice to the bulimic, it is to make yourself have breakfast. It'll stop you from nibbling snacks because you're hungry. If you think you can go without breakfast and then manage to skip lunch too, you'll find yourself really hungry by the evening and far more likely to binge. Admittedly I do have a fear that once I've got the taste of breakfast in my mouth I'm going to want more and more food. But I've just got to try and break the habit.

'I've always prayed throughout this, and I've got a friend who has been praying for me. I suppose I feel that I do want something dramatic to happen, but I know that it's not going to happen. My eating problem won't disappear overnight. The main thing for me to think on is that God wants me to be healed. He doesn't want me to be like this. I've just got to keep that perspective in sight.'

TANYA is in her late twenties. She looks back to her late teens when eating and not eating completely ruled her life for two and a half years. Like Ruth it was boy trouble that proved to be the catalyst. 'He told me that I was getting too fat, so

I started dieting, but before long I'd got it into my head that I was overweight even though I wasn't. It soon got to the stage where I began to feel guilty about eating, so I started making myself sick. My mother was obviously concerned and took me to the local GP, who didn't know what to think of me. But Mum also tried to ignore it. I think she hoped it would go away. She probably had her thoughts, but she didn't say anything, and no one else supposedly knew. I was down to seven stone from nine and a half stone, which for my height of five foot six, was quite a dramatic change.

'It was my own realization that something was wrong with me that helped me to get better. I was training to be a nurse and I can remember thinking that I should be in a psychiatric hospital. Like any addiction it is only by coming to terms that there's something wrong that you can start to improve. If you don't get to that stage it's hard to do anything about your condition.

'But physically I just wasn't the way I felt I should be; as magazines showed women to be. I'd always look at people and think "They look nice" and feel that I was an awful lot fatter than they were. Spiritually I found it a very hard time because I was a Christian, and Christians didn't do that sort of thing. I was at a loose end as far as church was concerned. My husband, Richie – who was the only person I got support from – and I prayed together and did a lot of studying about the body as the temple of the Holy Spirit which we're supposed to look after, and learnt that God loves you the way you are, mentally *and* physically. People with eating disorders need to realize that God loves them. Your self-esteem is so low and you don't love yourself – which is probably the main crux of the problem.

'When I confessed to Richie about my eating problems, we made a pact. He would keep an eye on me and try to make sure that I didn't make myself sick; he'd ask me how I was doing each day, and so I continue to make progress.

'But the Devil still throws all your troubles back in your face from time to time', she discloses. 'Maybe I'll have been out for a meal, and having got home I'll start feeling guilty, particularly at times when I feel low and under stress. But you can either tell Satan to go, or get caught up in it all again. Now I do feel I am in control, but every so often I have a lapse. Yet I don't feel I'll fall into the same trap of doing it all the time, especially after having had children; that definitely helped me because you then have to look after yourself and eat properly.

'I still get very touchy if people say things about people's weight', she admits. 'People need to be careful about the comments they make. They can hit hard and stick there. Even one of my two daughters has said that she's fat. There's such a pressure to look slim, and they're only five and seven years old.

'People suffering from eating disorders have to realize that they need to make some sort of confession, like in Alcoholics Anonymous, to come to terms with it. That's the first step, and then after that it gets easier to try and work it out of your system. You also need somebody really close to you to help and support you.

'If anybody had confronted me about my eating habits I would have denied it: "Don't be silly, I'm perfectly all right." But maybe if somebody had said, "I know what's wrong with you and I can help you. I'm here if you need me", I would have been more open. In a Christian context, one can pray for the chance to talk about it. It's so bad otherwise to end up in hospital.

'I don't know how I'd have coped if I'd been confined to bed. I don't know if that's the right way to go about it. In Christian circles people should realize what a person is going through before it gets to the stage where they have to be hospitalized. We need to get at the root of the problem, and away from the false image we have of what is a perfect woman.

'People can't be cured of eating disorders overnight. Victory is asking God to break Satan's power over it; there's a fine line between it being a spiritual or a physical problem, for what you look like is a very psychological issue. Eating disorders are an obsession of the mind, whereas addiction is more of a physical craving. I've certainly been made aware of the pressures on girls and women as I've watched my girls growing up.

'There's a lot of deceit involved; it's hard to tell people that you've been pretending, hiding food and throwing it up. There's a need for a lot more education, for people are not aware of the psychological effects. Eating disorders must be rampant.

I also went overboard on fitness at the same time as my eating problems. I already went to ballet twice a week, but upped the number to four or five classes; I was going swimming and playing hockey, I'd walk into town, and I wasn't eating. Even my ballet teacher mentioned that I was losing my strength. I still have a set of scales I have to use every day. And if I'm one pound over my normal weight then I can't eat my breakfast.'

'I was never a slight child. I was always "big-boned", as the saying goes', admits ALISON. 'It was when I was about eighteen I had a really bad break-up with a boyfriend and I was sure he'd want me back if I lost weight.'

Alison ended up anorexic for about a year: 'But it took me about a year and a half to recover. And then I went to the other extreme and became a compulsive eater, which I still am', she reveals.

'My grandmother brought up my sister and me. If something went wrong she'd comfort us with food. Everything became associated with food. My dad was a heavy man and he died of a heart attack. That really made me think; I was thirteen stone when he died and I soon got down to eleven.

'Most anorexics conceal what they're up to by wearing huge baggy jumpers, which I did', she admits. 'At my worst stage I was down to five and a half stone. But then I went to England from my home in Ireland to visit a close friend. I was in an emotional mess but she really helped me and my weight rocketed. I went from five and a half stone to thirteen and a half very quickly.

'I still love my food,' Alison admits, 'and I still struggle with my eating problem. I did get my weight down again, to eight and a half stone, at which I really felt confident. One friend commented that I shouldn't lose any more weight, but I did. At my lowest point I was just drinking one coffee a day. My hair was dull and listless, I had dark shadows under my eyes and my periods had stopped, as well as being exceptionally skinny. By rights I should have died.

'God certainly had His hand on me', she believes. 'I was a Christian, but when you're eighteen there's a tendency for people to be saved and then be left to their own devices. I've been a Christian for twenty-one years, but it's only since last year that I've started to grow in my faith.

'My main problem now is with my husband. He's six foot two with hollow legs, so he finds it difficult at times to understand my problem, and he thinks I'm more attractive when I'm thinner, but when you've had a weight problem as I have you're always aware of every pound you weigh.

'I'm very ruled by my emotions, but I've been very fortunate in having a close Christian friend who has really helped my self-esteem. She builds me up and meets a real need. Because of her support and love for me she has made me recognize my self-worth, she has made me see myself as a nice person. Very often compulsive eaters and anorexics don't love themselves, but I've come to understand that God loves me just the way I am.

'As far as my eating habits go, I enjoy the social

side of going out for a meal. Chinese food is a big weakness; and I'll manage to eat a meal with my husband, follow it up with some cheese later, as well as crisps and chocolate, and still not feel sick. I can consume great quantities of food; people sometimes say, "I'm absolutely stuffed", but I never feel full.

'I eat when I'm not hungry, so I can identify with compulsive eaters. I can recognize them. I'll often talk to people about food and they'll open up and tell me how they feel. I do wish somebody would say, "How are we going to stop this?" Even when I'm eating a healthy diet I still feel this need to eat, yet I know that food can't bring love, or fulfil one's feelings of insecurity that you're not loved by some people. In fact it makes you feel worse', she reveals.

'A lot of my problem is associated with greed. I am greedy, I have a big appetite, but at the same time that's something that God can deal with in me. Gluttony *is* a sin. I'm especially greedy for sweets and chocolate, the sweeter it is the better I like it.

'When I lost two stone and bought myself a new dress, people said that I looked really slim and elegant, and that I must have a lot of will-power. But when they weren't there I'd eat. They didn't know what was going on. But while you can hide in the food cupboard, you can't hide from God, He's in the cupboard with you! He knows what you're scoffing.

'I now find that I do the same things with my children as my grandmother did with me. I'll say,

"Let's have a biscuit". They're aged eight and four so I do make an effort to encourage them to eat fruit or crisps when they're hungry instead of sweets.

'Being in control of my weight is not so much about being on a calorie-controlled diet all the time. It's about learning to love yourself. I do feel more confident when I'm thinner, and more accepted. It can be a vicious circle at times, but I'm gradually learning to be in control of my eating habits.

'Sometimes when the children say that they're starving my husband tends to reply, "You're not starving". That's the thing about the whole issue of food. There's those images of weak babies hanging on to their mothers' breast for want of milk, but we mentally switch off. We can help by saying to our children: "You're not starving. You're hungry, but you're not starving." '

ALAN, the sole man among those I questioned, is a thin, athletic looking figure. A quiet man, as he relates the experiences of his eating disorder, one can't help noticing the gold crowns that line his teeth. 'I both vomited and scavenged', he admits. 'I also starved myself; being below six stone is quite serious for a five foot ten person. The whole ordeal lasted over eight years, and I had eight hospital admissions in the space of five years', he candidly reveals.

'At university I did a lot of boxing and had to keep my weight down, so I had to be very careful about what I ate, and I started to be able to make myself sick. My health did settle down for a year or so, but then I got married, and on the wedding night my wife declared that she hadn't wanted to go through with it. We had a four-week trial period, but the marriage was never consummated. When my wife then left me I went totally to pieces; it was a tunnel from which I thought I'd never get out. It got to the stage where I couldn't hold down food and I was rushed to hospital after collapsing in the street. I ended up in a psychiatric wing', he discloses.

'I was a Christian all through my experience, and in fact being an evangelical Christian doesn't necessarily help. People don't always know what to say, and I felt it was a sin that I couldn't exercise enough self-control, but it was also something I just couldn't do anything about.

'I ended up in the Royal Edinburgh Hospital and there had a counselling relationship with the chaplain. I wasn't convinced that helped, but it was good to have somebody I could talk to, because although my university friends stuck by me and my family are very long-suffering, both were in different parts of the country, so I felt fairly isolated during my illness.

'Though intellectually you know God loves you and you know very well what you're doing to yourself and that your feelings of guilt are not justified, you nevertheless have to start to feel valued again. It's also important to get some structure to your life. I ended up teaching in a boarding school where I knew meals were available and where I was working with other people. You've got to be sensible. If you're going to live alone or live an isolated life, then that's silly. You've got to be sensible about strategy and tactics if you want to stay well. It's important, too, to find somebody with whom you can relate and relax, and who will love you and stay with you.

'People do come out of it, but because I was a man, people didn't know how to deal with me. Because my anorexia was severe and prolonged, I really believe that the doctors had given up on me. I feel that God held me and brought me out of my troubles, and if you can find someone to stand with you, don't keep it to yourself, for goodness sake.

'Anorexia by itself is a symptom of depression, because when you're below weight, you're active but you're tired, and you feel the cold terribly. Winter is a far worse time for anorexics, and they get all the symptoms of depression; not being able to sleep, waking up at two a.m. and feeling suicidal. Many will carry it out if their illness is prolonged.

'But there's not a standard as to what an anorexic will be like, though many teenage girls do get it', Alan admits. 'Yet what is common to them all is that they need help and advice and to be able to get the whole thing out of their system. It's hopeless to deal with just one aspect of the problem.

'People recovering from anorexia first need to put on weight to stop them from collapsing in the street or having a heart attack, but it's very important to deal with the social, psychological and maybe spiritual aspects at the same time. Anorexia is a multi-faceted problem and there's no point in just treating the symptoms in the hope that it'll keep the person afloat for the next two years and they'll just happen to pass out of that phase.

'Anorexics go on the defensive and automatically deny that they're suffering from it, which just makes them more devious. One's self-image is totally distorted, yet you have to recognize that you are suffering from a long-term problem, and you have to get to the root of the problem. It is very important that the anorexic is persuaded that they need help', he stresses.

'On the whole, people who become anorexic have a lot of drive and tend to punish themselves; that's an enormous force once it's properly harnessed. They must be helped to see that there's hope on the horizon, for most people do initially feel that there's no hope.

'Eighteen months before everything came to a head for me I had gone to my GP, complaining that I was being sick and that I couldn't sleep at night and was walking for hours in the middle of the night. And he just said, "You're worrying too much, take a holiday". . . .

'Anorexics do develop a lot of psychological problems because there's the denial, loss of emotion, and feelings which need to be worked out. The Church doesn't help by often expecting us to conform to a particular outward appearance of behaviour. Certain things, such as anorexia, tend not to be on the agenda for discussion. And it is decidedly not helpful for people to talk about carrying out exorcisms. Fair enough if people want to pray for you, but some churches should carry a government health warning.

'These days, I'm healthy though I still don't eat much fattening food. I'm very conscious of Third World needs and work for a Third World charity, but life is there to be enjoyed and that is for everybody. I'd say to any anorexic, "Don't think you're special, that God's grace isn't good enough for you, and that you should keep the punishment to yourself." '

Action station

- Read:
    The Beauty Myth by Naomi Wolf (Vintage 1991)
    Fat is a Feminist Issue by Susie Orbach (Arrow Books)
    Rosemary Conley's Complete Hip and Thigh Diet by Rosemary Conley (Arrow 1989)
    Dying to be Thin by Elizabeth Round (Lion 1990)
    Anorexia Nervosa and Bulimia: how to help by M. Duker and R. Slade (Open University Press)

- For information and practical advice about eating disorders contact the Christian group Anorexia and Bulimia Care, 15 Fernhurst Gate, Aughton, Ormskirk, Lancs L39 5ED.

- Write to the Health Education Authority, Hamilton House, Mabledon Place, London WC1H 9TX for information about healthy eating, including the brochure *Beating heart disease*.

- Whatever your size or weight, make a point of taking regular exercise to keep yourself physically fit and well-toned to do God's work.

3
Celebrate the Feast

Not only is Christianity a communal religion, one that cannot survive without people coming together to worship and share themselves, but at its very heart is the simple yet profound sharing of the bread and wine to symbolize the ultimate celebration. Broken and drunk as Jesus said 'in remembrance of me'[1] its stark simplicity is a potent symbol of Jesus' victory over death.

Over the centuries the Church has developed an elaborate array of festivals to commemorate significant moments in the life of Christ. Palm Sunday, Good Friday, Easter and Christmas are the highlights of the Christian year, but there are a wealth of other dates to celebrate that can be traced back to Old Testament times. And of course attending church on a Sunday, the day of Jesus' resurrection, is a weekly reminder of what He accomplished for us.

As far back as Moses' time the Israelites honoured God by keeping an annual harvest festival in which a tenth of what they produced – grain, wine, oil and even newborn animals – was set aside for a huge feast. And if an individual lived too far away to be able to carry all that produce and meat, it could be converted into money to buy whatever was needed for the party once they got there. 'Use the silver to buy whatever you like; cattle, sheep, wine or other fermented drink, or anything you wish. Then you and your household shall eat there in the presence of the Lord your God and rejoice.'[2]

Even though the nativity celebration is high on the agenda in the Christian Church, it's easy to be critical about the extravagance of Christmas. It's been over-commercialized to the extent that Jesus just doesn't figure in many families' celebrations, and children can grow up without a knowledge of what it's really all about. In some primary schools, where everyone's very quick to remember the Muslim, Sikh and Jewish festivals for the multi-racial children in their charge, when it comes to Christmas, it's Santa who gets all the limelight.

As Christians it's up to us to emphasize Jesus' position at the heart of the traditional celebrations. Many make a point of only sending cards that illustrate an aspect of the Bible story of Jesus' birth. It's a time to open your home to those without family or friends, and express the joy of knowing Jesus with them too.

Understandably not every Christian is happy with the commercialization of our special days. Some suggest, as the Puritans did before us, that we remove all the trappings and focus solely on the Gospel story. Others suggest we shift the date of Christmas to another time of the year, and leave 25th December to the heathens. It's a fair argument, yet as things stand at the moment we have a tremendous opportunity to share our faith at a time of the year when people are particularly open to the Gospel. Attending Midnight Mass on Christmas Eve or the Family Service on the following morning is a tradition for Christians and non-Christians across the land.

Custom or ritual has a strong role within communities of any size be they family, school, church or work place. It is a shared history that knits people together. For example, most of us, if we cast our minds back, can recognize family tradition in the way we celebrate birthdays, Christmas and other special occasions that have developed over the years. Many will be connected with food. Christmas wouldn't be Christmas for me without my mum's homemade Christmas pud and a slice of her cake. At our childhood birthday parties she would also come up with ingenious ways of presenting party fare. She would make Cybermats (the Cyberman equivalent of Dr Who's K9) out of flat loaves of bread with sausages on sticks sticking out of the sides. As my sister's birthday is a day before Guy Fawkes Night, one year Mum concocted a miniature 'bonfire' out of macaroni, added a few sausages, and sat the father figure from our dolls' house on top. The creativity runs in the family. Jane and a friend once 'painted' a massive tongue on the top of a birthday cake for a friend who was a Rolling Stones fan. But apparently the birthday girl's mother was so horrified that she nearly threw it in the bin!

There's certainly ways to be very creative with

food that at the same time take account of the potential joy it brings others. Through a simple meal together or by giving something of ourselves through the gift of some food, we emphasize its celebratory nature. God's great gift of food to us gains an added dimension when we follow His example and use it to bring us close to others.

Any excuse for a party

The more we get into recognizing that the Christian life is a celebration of the hope we have in Jesus, the more joyful we feel and ready to share ourselves and our home with others. After all, Heaven throws a party for every sinner who turns to Christ![3] Celebration is part of our Christian heritage.

It starts from inviting friends round and providing them with cups of tea and simple meals to literally opening your home. And parties just happen. It's a mirror of Jesus' distinct statement that 'when two or three are gathered together in my name, I will be there'.[4] For Christians who invite friends round, the truth is that Jesus is right there with them preparing the ground and arranging all the details, right down to the seating plan!

The late Salvation Army leader Catherine Bramwell-Booth had a mischievous streak that ran throughout her life, and she was a great party-giver for friends and family. 'As well as birthdays, Christmas and New Year, they also celebrated the shortest day of the year, the longest day of the year, Leap Year and anything else that turned up on the calendar.'[5]

Maybe you don't feel you're much of a party animal. Start small and see what happens. As people get older they enjoy sitting round and having a good old chinwag. Heck, I can bop with the best of them, though it's getting to the stage when I remember all the cover versions and reissues from the first time around. Minnie Ripperton's 'Loving You' was the first song that ever made me cry, when I was all of junior school age. The last party I went to I was the only one jiggling about to The Stranglers' 'No More Heroes' because the others couldn't really get into it. I felt terribly old. . . .

One of the two big parties I've organized for friends of all ages was designed in two parts so that the afternoon 'garden party' catered for the older and quieter ones or those with children, and the evening disco was planned for everyone else to let their hair down. As it happened, the disco didn't materialize, because everyone was happy enough to sit around and natter. The whole 'do' was very low-key, but very successful nevertheless.

It was also relatively very cheap. My biggest expense was mailing out the home-made invites. The cards and reused envelopes cost me nothing, but the stamps came to quite a bit! I just asked everybody to bring some savoury or sweet food so that I didn't only end up with crisps and peanuts, and so there would also be enough for everybody, with very little left over. It worked.

There are certainly plenty of Christian festivals throughout the year for us to celebrate, but there are other anniversaries and special days too that can provide the opportunity for gathering people together to have a good time, and by which you can also serve Jesus. Theme diaries and calendars are very useful for providing you with details of special dates. Not only does my 'Trees for Life' diary give me the dates of full moons (I always get a bit of a growl in my throat around those times) and the major Christian festivals, but it also announces World Food Day (16th October), the date the sea eagle was successfully reintroduced to Scotland (31st July 1985), and Live Aid (13th July 1985), as well as the sadder environmental events of history such as the Bhopal chemical disaster in India (2nd December 1984), the murder of Brazilian rubber tapper and rainforest activist Chico Mendes (22nd December 1988) and the extinction of the Tasmanian tiger on 7th September 1936. Such a diary prompts me to party *and* to pray.

Yet we should be on the look-out for excuses to party every day of our lives. As Christians we should have a mischievous glint in our eye and an attitude to life that surprises people and lifts their spirits. Food in this respect is a great catalyst. In most work places, on somebody's birthday it's customary for the birthday person to treat everyone to sticky buns or whatever. In some offices everybody goes out for a meal together to celebrate. And your food giving can be spontaneous too. If you're visiting a friend and happen to be passing a baker's, pop in for a couple of cakes or ginger-bread men to munch with your mate over a pot of tea. If you're going out to a film or getting a video in, see if there's a food connection that you can home in on for an idea of what to eat that evening. *Babette's Feast* is a great foodie film, though perhaps a bit too adventurous for most cooks. If you're watching *Twin Peaks* re-runs make yourself a 'damn fine' cup of coffee and a real cherry pie to savour just the way Coop does. My mate Jane and I happened to pop into a pasta bar before we went to see *The Fly*. We were glad that we'd eaten before the film. Having seen a man turn horrific-ally into a massive housefly and do the things that flies are wont to do with their food, I doubt I'd have been able to face the sauce that had been so liberally ladled all over our spaghetti. . . . And don't go for a pizza after watching *Betty Blue* either.

Making a meal of it

Because God has provided the food we eat, celeb-rating the feast should stretch to the apparently run-of-the-mill meals as much as when it's party time. That's why saying Grace is such a good idea; because it brings this very fact to the forefront of our thoughts.

What you eat first thing in the morning sets you up for the rest of the day. Admittedly many people find it difficult to stomach more than a cup of black coffee before they leave for work or school, but it's questionable how effective they'll be in the morning on an empty stomach. Indeed, going without food for more than three hours causes a drop in blood sugar level which results in tiredness and lack of concentration. Coffee is one of those substances that, like chocolate, will only boost energy temporarily and then leave you feeling worse than you felt before! If you haven't time for a proper breakfast, grab a piece of fruit instead.

I'm a three-courser myself when I'm organized enough, and I found a proper breakfast was particularly useful when I was an impoverished student. Having eaten a good solid breakfast I found I could get by with the minimum lunch. If I'd accidentally slept in and didn't have time for breakfast I'd boil myself an egg, make a marmalade sandwich out of my slice of toast, and eat it on the hoof instead. My family was brought up on proper breakfasts; it was a good way of getting the clan together before we set off for school. My mother also ingeniously used it as a gauge if any of us had declared that we weren't in a fit state to go to school; if we were well enough to eat breakfast of cornflakes, scrambled egg and a slice of toast to follow, her logic decided that we were well enough for studies!

Make a point of being sociable with your meals. Lunchtimes when you're working or studying can be one of the few times you'll get to do some reading or writing letters. If you're a bit of a solitary creature by nature it can be easy to get along without those with whom you share your day. Balance out your moments of solitude with time spent among colleagues. Use the shared time of lunchtime to extend friendship to those around you. When you're at home at the end of the day, do the same. Many people do sit down together as a family to eat in the evening, but if you don't, share the food you make for yourself with another. Use your food to strengthen family ties.

As well as thanking God through prayer at meal times for the food in front of you, each time you eat show your love in action by putting aside some money for those who are forced to go without. UNICEF has its own Jar of Grace Appeal which works on this very basis to support projects among the children of the Third World. It acts as a constant reminder at meal times of how fortunate we are to live as we do, and how being in that position should motivate us to do something for others.

It is an opportunity too to develop our own knowledge and experience of the richness of the Judeo-Christian tradition.

People can be scathing about tradition and ritual, but it adds structure to our lives in a memorable way. Many Christians neglect the Old Testament, since it's the part of the Bible that confuses them when it comes to its relevance to being a Christian. Yet within its pages are not only the story of the trials and tribulations of a people, but also of celebrations and feastings offered to God with deep gratitude for how He had helped the Jews.

And that celebration is as much part of Christian heritage as it is of Jewish heritage. Not only does awareness of this enhance our Christian life and culture, but it brings Jew and Gentile together in mutual worship of the Father, which is an added dimension to God's rich provision. I still gratefully recall from my childhood days the kindness of the local Jewish councillor who gave up what must have been some of her much-valued spare time to show a bunch of Sunday School children the variety of foods that Jews used in their festivals. Unfortunately all I can remember of the occasion is not being very struck by the rather dry and tasteless unleavened bread, though the woman's very presence at that church, with her assortment of foodstuffs, had much to say about how much Christians have to learn of the art of celebrating our faith.

Action station

- Read:

    We Always Put A Candle In The Window by Marjorie Freeman (National Society/Church House Publishing 1989)

    Feasting For Festivals by Jan Wilson (Lion 1990)

    Christmas – And Always: celebrating through the year by Rita Snowden (Fount 1989)

    Celebration: the book of Jewish festivals edited by Naomi Black (Collins 1987)

    The Kingdom of God is a Party by Tony Campolo (Word 1990)

    A Body Broken For A Broken People by Francis J. Maloney (Collins Dove 1990)

- For details of UNICEF's Jar of Grace Appeal, write to: UNICEF, 55 Lincoln's Inn Fields, London WC2A 3NB.

- Make sure you sit down for a meal at least once a day. Whether with others or on your own, take time to enjoy the occcasion.

- When you hold a party be sure to invite people outside your immediate circle of friends. Look out for the less popular ones at school or work and make a point of befriending them.

5
Eating Out

It's often a cross between convenience, laziness and just a need for a change of scene and atmosphere that prompts people to eat out. Artists Gilbert and George apparently have only an electric kettle at their home-cum-studio. Otherwise they eat at a local homely caff. And I once read of a woman who, sick of taking hours preparing a good meal for dinner party guests, preferred entertaining at a local restaurant, having calculated that the cost of treating her friends to a meal there wasn't much greater than at her home; and she didn't have to do the washing up afterwards.

All this writing about food certainly makes me very hungry. I've eaten out far more while I've been writing this book than usual. It just seems too much hassle to worry not only about what I'm going to eat, but the buying, preparation and cooking of meals too. Instead I've got into the habit of hot-footing it along to my local Wimpy, Pizzaland or Burger King (that's Hounslow haute cuisine for you) before heading home to work on this book. Purely for research purposes, you understand. Interestingly enough, it's got to the stage where I've had it up to the eyeballs with french fries and spicy beanburgers, and my body craves fresh fruit, unadulterated vegetables and something basic like a boiled egg. Oh, the joy of eating a massive cheese salad!

For there's a point where we as Christians should stop to think about our eating habits. Admittedly there's not a lot in the Bible about buying a meal. But there's certainly a pattern for eating out in a general sense. Experiences of Jesus and His disciples include sharing food among the crowds that followed them: ' "I have compassion for those people; they have already been with me three days and have nothing to eat" . . . He told the crowd to sit down on the ground. When He had taken the seven loaves and given thanks, He broke them and gave them to His disciples to set before the people, and they did so. They had a few small fish as well; He gave thanks for them also and told the disciples to distribute them. The people ate and were satisfied.'[1]

And eating at others' homes: 'While Jesus was having dinner at Levi's house, many tax collectors and "sinners" were eating with Him and His disciples, for there were many who followed Him. When the teachers of the law who were Pharisees saw Him eating with the "sinners" and tax collectors, they asked His disciples, "Why does He eat with tax collectors and sinners?" On hearing this, Jesus said to them, "It is not the healthy who need a doctor, but the sick. I have not come to call the righteous, but sinners." '[2]

Both episodes point to some trends that we

should heed. Though Jesus had His solitary moments alone with God, when He was with His disciples or the crowds and individuals He responded with compassion and directness to their needs. He looked out for other people – and so should we. So if He and His disciples had been around today and popped into a restaurant for a meal, the party wouldn't stop at their large table, but ripple out to adjacent tables so that others could join in the fun. Though personally I'd trust that they'd be more civil and thoughtful than, say, a bunch of painfully loutish Hooray Henrys or lager-swilling soul boys. In the same way that Heaven is an open house to those who believe in Jesus, He would welcome all who came to His table.

If you've ever stopped to listen to someone over a meal, you'll be aware of how easy it is to get so engrossed in the conversation that you forget your meal. I can well imagine Jesus listening to people around Him asking His advice, with Him barely having a chance to sample a morsel of His meal. In the same way we should try not to be too exclusive with our meals – though it's nice to celebrate a birthday, new job or whatever anniversary among friends, as Jesus shared His day with His disciples apart from the crowd. But if, as most people, you have friends from different departments of your life, say church, work, school or college, encourage cross-over by inviting friends from church over to enjoy a meal out with friends from your school life. Break down barriers over a meal out.

Bring these principles into café society and we

soon realize that at a fundamental level many restaurants are élitist. The type of place that turns its nose up at certain people we should bypass, for anything divisive, by its very nature, cannot be Christian. But at the same time, don't be put off giving top class places a try out. If they're as classy as they appear, they shouldn't mind what you look like as long as you can afford to pay your bill. In the film *Breakfast at Tiffany's* there's a very humorous and touching scene where Audrey Hepburn and her male friend pop into the famous jewellery store to buy something. But the only thing that they can afford in the opulent store is to have something engraved: only they can't afford any of the expensive jewellery to engrave a message on. But they do have a cheap 'out of a cracker' ring, so the man behind the counter graciously accepts that and has it decorated for them. He treats this cheap couple as if they were his best customers. And any restaurant worth its salt will do that too.

And don't be put off by the 'not for the likes of me' attitude that some people have. March in as if you own the place – but not in an arrogant manner; just hold your head up high. After all, you have as much right to eat there as anyone else. 'For John came neither eating nor drinking, and they say, "He has a demon". The Son of Man came eating and drinking, and they say, "Here is a glutton and a drunkard, a friend of tax collectors and sinners". But wisdom is proved by her actions.'[3]

My mother tells me of the time that she and her

nursing friends went hostelling during the Fifties and ended up weary and hungry at a rather nice hotel. (For future reference, any decent place they found to eat on their travels, they'd mark on their OS map with a capital T.) Clad in their muddy walking boots they were obviously aware that it probably wasn't the done thing to go marching into the dining room leaving trails of footprints across carpets and tile floors. 'Would you like us to take our boots off?', my mum courteously enquired. 'If madam would feel more comfortable without them', was the waiter's dignified reply!

Foreign affair

We British are an insular lot. In the same way that we're reluctant to learn foreign languages, feeling that it's *them* who should bother to learn English, we like our food native too. So whether we eat out here or abroad we're not known for being adventurous. True, maybe we'll stretch to conveyor belt pizzas or plastic tacos, but when it comes to the real thing we tend to hold back.

Which is a great shame. In cities in particular there's a wealth of cuisine from overseas to try. Many large towns have areas where people of particular nationalities tend to gather. It's here that you should be able to experience real home cooking. A good bench mark, if you're not sure how good a place is, is to see whether it's being visited by natives of the country its food represents. I doubt you'll find many Italians in your local pizza house (there was once an American kid who on holiday in Italy turned to his father and remarked, 'Gee, Dad, they have pizzas here too!' . . .) Check out the *real* Italian restaurants instead.

As Christians it is surely our responsibility, if we live in an area with a high population of people of other races and cultures, to get to know them. In Hounslow there's a large Asian community. A mate of mine, Jenny, a post mistress, has made it her job to learn Punjabi. Not only has she made friends with a lot of the Asians on her round, but she finds it very useful when she and her husband Neil visit local Indian restaurants. She chatters away to the staff and there've been times when they've been treated to a free dish! Because my father grew up in India, my family has been used to eating curries for decades. Not only would Mum concoct them at home, but we'd frequent Indian restaurants too. Now that we've all but flown the nest, when all six of us do manage to be in the same place at the same time we tend to congregate at the local tandoori. As a vegetarian I continue to enjoy eating Indian and appreciate too the quiet atmosphere of the eating houses. It's my favourite foreign food.

Food can become a way of uniting people from across the world. Make yourself familiar with not only the food but the ways of eating peculiar to different countries. In the UK we 'pile' food on to the back of our forks, in the US the fork is used more like a spoon. In Asia curries are scooped into the mouth in pieces of chapati. Chopsticks are the tools of the Orient. My friend Sally's brother Andrew is teaching English as a foreign language

(TEFL) in Japan. Tall, blond and obviously Western, he causes quite a stir wherever he goes. But when, like his companions, he picks up a pair of chopsticks and is able to use them as well, everybody stops and stares!

It's a shame that good British meals out tend to be expensive; it's difficult to share our own rich food culture with others when we eat out. Nevertheless, we *can* share ourselves with others from different worlds. Being adventurous enough to try food from other cultures and countries can be the first step on the way to opening ourselves up to learning about other places, their politics and their people. The difference in taste and recipes is all part of that great creative process that God began and shared with us. At a very basic level, common to all humankind is the God-given gift to create. Food from across the world, and the way similar ingredients are often used and adapted imaginatively and originally to suit national tastes and needs, reveals that great truth.

Slap-up meal

Some places are just prohibitively expensive for all but the most wealthy of eaters. And some people will always eat well while others starve or live in poor conditions. During wartime, while East-Enders crowded into the dark, dank and insanitary London Underground system for shelter from the bombing, the well-to-do continued to live it up at the Savoy. So much for all pulling together! And it was quite intriguing recently to watch society chef Marco Pierre White and TV host Jonathon Ross smugly agree between themselves that £150 wasn't much to spend on an evening meal out for two, while the Jonathon Ross Show audience – probably largely made up of the student/young trendy/Time Out crowd – gasped in shock, and you could almost hear them thinking 'Crumbs, we get by on a tenner each!'

There must be some point where the amount of money spent on food becomes obscene. After all, how much can people comfortably eat in one sitting? The Romans used to lounge around in their tricliniums, filling themselves up on rich delicacies, and would then take emetics to make themselves sick so that they could begin their eating all over again . . . ; institutionalized bulimia. Who said they were a civilized bunch?

The cost of eating out often strikes me as having distinct parallels with the cost of getting your hair cut. The sky might be the limit in the cost you *could* pay, but actually there's a limit to what you can do with the basic ingredients before you adulterate and ruin the whole effect, whether that's hair or food. It certainly showed itself up in the consumer-boom Eighties when people with more money than sense paid mightily for scraps of food arranged exotically but rather minimalistically and termed 'nouvelle cuisine'. I'm sure there's a moral in there somewhere – that the worth and status, when put in terms of how much money people earned, was in reality not worth a morsel . . . A piece of bread literally bought a sack of gold.

Café society

We haven't yet got our café scene as organized as the French, but stopping for 'a cup of tea and a bun' in the midst of your travels is a tradition passed down particularly through generations of women. It's a chance to take a breather halfway through a shopping spree or when gallery hopping to catch up on news.

It was in the Fifties when the coffee bar really came into its own, and girls *and* lads met over nothing stronger than watered down caffeine. You can still get a proper cuppa and relax over the Sunday papers, but it's a dying art. Increasingly the chink of china is being replaced by the flakiness of moulded polystyrene beakers. And strangely enough, though it *seems* all very futuristic, these throwaway bright white cups, plastic teaspoons, dunk-it-yourself tea bags and flick-a-switch boilers, all have the depressingly opposite effect. There's something dreadfully primitive – and extortionate – about being handed all this para-phernalia, not forgetting the carton of UHT milk, and being expected to put it all together yourself.

Once waiting for a train at Euston BR station I was in the mood for a coffee, but I couldn't face the over-packaged and over-priced travellers' fare. I wandered a few hundred yards down the road and round the corner from Euston Square tube station I popped into Gino's coffee bar. It was like going back in time. Some of the original Fifties decor still remained, and the proprietors, having served tea, came and sat out among the customers and watched the passersby from their little corner of the world. The whole experience was much more pleasurable than anything I could have hoped for on the station concourse.

Churches and Christian bookshops increasingly are able to offer the same; it's a very good way of reaching out to people in the community who need a bit of a prompt to get through a church door. My own church, Holy Trinity in Hounslow, is smack bang in the middle of the busy High Street. Its very own Bridge bookshop and accompanying café acts like a magnet to tired shoppers. Because it's staffed by volunteers (one of the Church's most valuable resources) and serves home-made cakes and rolls alongside brand names, it's able to keep prices down and so draw in the locals. A business-woman friend of mind tells me that it's *the* place to go for Hounslow's business community because it's so cheap. Tracts at each table are there if visitors wish to know what this church business is all about. . . .

Of course, a coffee at the end of the service is an established event at most churches these days. Mind you, I've heard of one 'house church' where everybody begins the evening with doughnuts *before* the service, like some strange sort of *Twin Peaks* ritual, and another *rather* upper-middle-class church where tea was replaced by glasses of sherry. Which is overdoing it a bit, and rather alienating for anybody walking in off the street, one would imagine.

Fast and loose

Fast food is very much the popular downmarket end of the eating out business. These places are not exactly cheap, but there's a definite air of forced cheerfulness about them. A relatively recent innovation (many are only now celebrating twenty something anniversaries), they've revolutionized the way we regard eating out, and also the amount we're prepared to spend on a snack.

Across London there was at one time a network of cheap sandwich bars. They could be recognized by their detailed boards listing the plethora of filling combinations they could put between two slices of bread. They haven't completely disappeared (though I still lament the destruction of the one inside Baker Street tube station in London, with its tiled Brief Encounterish style interior and a fine line in cream cheese and pineapple filled rolls . . .), but many have been priced out of the market by the onslaught of the fast food palaces.

Certainly fast food restaurants are dependable places. You can be in any high street in the land – and in other lands, come to that – and you'll know exactly what to expect. In the same way that it used to be said (I don't know if it's true now) that the French education system was so finely tuned that on any given day the President could know what page of a set book a particular age group were working on, you can be sure that when you bite into your Macburger, there'll be countless others across the world doing exactly the same.

It is this bland uniformity, and also the complete

reluctance to take account of local tastes and culture, that is so stifling. McDonalds is often regarded as one of the biggest culprits. I recall a *Punch* cartoon from many years ago showing Tarzan flying happily through the jungle only to find himself rather perplexingly hanging from one of the 'humps' of a massive yellow M! As Ben Elton has remarked, people are killed trying to get over walls to freedom and for standing up for their beliefs. But at the slightest chink in the oppressor's armour, Ronald McDonald the clown goes bouncing in. And if it's not McDonalds, it'll be Burger King, Wimpy or a pizza house. The brash primary coloured façades take no account of local architecture, and the packaging that the food is wrapped in is a terrible waste of God's resources. In the mid–seventies my school mates and I went Red Bus Rovering around London (for the grand sum of 25p we had the freedom of the capital's buses) and ended up at a McDonalds. It was all a relatively new and exciting experience, but even as a twelve- or thirteen-year-old I was singularly unimpressed with the lack of cutlery and the egg carton style of packaging that held our burgers.

Recently McDonalds came under fire for using CFC-producing cartons. Teenage Americans, concerned about the potential damage to the environment, threatened to boycott the company's eateries if it didn't change its ways by a specific date. Realizing the potential loss of customers, McDonalds sensibly obliged. . . . That was quite a positive way that young people showed their consumer power; they'd turned the tables on a business that is so very much geared to the young.

Just by glancing round a fast food bar it's easy to tell that the whole atmosphere is very youthful. Burger King even has its own Kid's Club 'for the totally cool'! 'Fill in a form and you get the Super Official Totally Secret Membership Kit – free – with a bunch of wicked surprises' it says on its publicity bumpf. These places know that if you attract the kids (one wonders whatever happened to children), their parents are sure to cough up the readies. It seems that there will always be parents who are twisted round the little fingers of their offspring. Yet many teenagers also find that fast food bars have a magnetic attraction and are a great meeting place for when they're out on the town.

But the apparent convenience of filling up on double decker burgers, french fries and creamy milk shakes, contrasts horribly with the impact such eating habits make on vast tracts of the world's rain forests and the people and creatures native to the area. Admittedly, the beef cattle which fill the burgers in this country are not reared on rain forest land, but burger companies which trade in the UK are very much connected with the destruction of the lush environment of Central and South America. To produce a single hamburger, five square metres of grazing land is needed to feed the cow. In Honduras, the rain forest is being replaced by grassland and arid soil at such a rate that it could all but vanish within a decade. The beef is sold in the US to make fast food hamburgers, and Honduras earns valuable dollars in return. But the soil beneath the rain forest is fragile, and once stripped of its tropical canopy is barren within three years. Grass no longer grows and the cattle ranchers must drive their herds to new pastures, destroying more of the forest as they go.

Staff moral

When we eat away from home it's not just the issue of food we should consider, but the way the staff are treated too. Catering is a notoriously badly paid and uncomfortable career. The chef may appear all sweetness and light out in the restaurant, but he can become a tyrant behind the swing doors, ordering the kitchen staff about furiously. It's not so great for the waiting staff either. Often rushed off their feet, where once they used to get tips put aside for their troubles, these days more often than not, the service charge is included in the bill (no matter how bad the service). Not only is the choice taken away from the customer (and tipping *is* a choice; you should never feel that you should have to tip the person who's served you) but the 'tip' rarely goes to the waiter. Instead it is creamed off as part of the restaurant chain's profits.

Nevertheless, there's an increasing move among waiting staff to make themselves noticeable. It's not just the 'Are you enjoying your meal?' coupled with the generally desperate and insincere smile. There's a creeping Americanization that I find distinctly worrying. At one place I ate at in Kingston, the waiters did magic tricks and knelt at your table to look upwards into your face to ask what you wanted! When I enquired of one waiter why he had to go into this over-friendly mode, he jumped back and stood stiffly, notebook and pencil poised to take my order as if that was the English way of doing things. I don't know whether the waiters think they're going to get a bigger tip if they put on an act. I'm sure I'm not the only one for whom it has the opposite effect. If I go out for a meal with someone, on the whole I want to be left in peace. I don't mind exchanging pleasantries and maybe having a chat at the end of a meal, particularly if the waiter is from overseas. Indeed, as Christians, it's important that we're always ready to be open to individuals, but that doesn't mean we have to be falsely 'nice'. And I don't want to be forced into being friendly!

Whenever I eat at the Festival Hall on London's South Bank I'm always very aware that most of the waiting staff are black. I'm sure that someone could argue that the company concerned has a positive discrimination policy for black employees. That's one way of looking at it. To me, it feels like I'm eating at the Cotton Club. Many fast food places work on a similar basis. Particularly in larger cities you'll notice that most of the staff don't speak a great deal of English. One gets the impression that these places are practically their first port of call when they enter the country. At least they're getting jobs, one could say, but they're also grotty, low-paid and tough.

An acquaintance of mine told me how he'd worked for a number of years in a restaurant which boasted Elizabeth Taylor and Joan Collins amongst its clientele. Consequently he raked in the tips, which boosted his pay no end. But the downside was that the work was so exhausting that all the staff took 'speed' to keep going. Personally, regardless of the Christian teaching on taking drugs, I've always been of the persuasion that if you need to take anything to keep going, whether that's amphetamines, alcohol, ginseng or doses of pure caffeine, then the job's not worth the effort.

On the take

I've got into the habit of visiting my local chippie once a week, usually on a Friday when the work week has ended, and I've got to know the staff to the extent that when I pass the place on my way into Hounslow I generally get a wave. Other people have a restaurant where they're known; I'm a bit more downmarket. (Until it recently closed down, I also had a discount at my local Sue Ryder store, I was such a good customer. Other people get discounts at Harrods. . . .)

But with this take-away business I find myself very concerned about what my chips are wrapped in. A few years ago the *NME* had a great and very trendy slogan 'Wrap your chips in nothing else'. The days of newspaper wrapping seem long past. These days you're fortunate if you get proper chips. More often than not they're those dreadful french fries that just don't have the same *je ne sais quoi*. Part of the enjoyment of chip eating is unwrapping the paper to be hit by a waft of vinegar that leaves you gasping for air.

One of the worst problems with take-away food is the sheer amount of litter it leaves in its wake. Unfortunately people are less concerned about taking away the wrappers. Not just chip papers, but polystyrene moulded cartons and boxes from fast food emporia ruin the environment and show up very clearly our lax attitudes towards the resources God has given us. If you're going to take away, be choosy about where you buy it from. Avoid the plastic coated palaces. Instead head for the cardboard covered centres. Both Burger King and Pizzaland provide cardboard containers for their food. Indeed, Pizzaland uses material that is '100 per cent dioxin-free pulp and is biodegradable and recyclable'. I read that on the side of my pizza box. Only trouble is, I didn't have a clue where I could take it to be recycled so it ended up in the bin. I felt OK about that. The box had a Keep Britain Tidy Group bin logo on the side too.

But try not to get too reliant on take-aways. They're not the best way to eat, socialize or spend your money. And though it's very tempting after a long day to grab a pizza and perhaps a video and crash out in front of the box with your 1.5 litre bottle of Coke (that's all my local pizza take-away sells), it's not the ideal way to spend an evening. It's an isolating way to live that can separate us from friends, and the need for God.

However, on a good day you can extend the whole idea of take-aways to going for a picnic with friends. And you don't have to pay your way to such an extent either. Instead, make up a batch of sandwiches and bring along a cool, refreshing drink to share with the others. Picnics are a great way to show how teamwork and pooling your resources can prove much more exciting than doing things individually. Try to avoid bringing with you anything that will end up as rubbish. Use packed lunch boxes and flasks or plastic bottles that can be used again and again. Remember to leave the area where you eat in the same condition as, if not better than, you found it. The organization 'Greener Gifts' has come up with an ingenious way to raise money to plant trees across the country's counties. People who want to picnic on the banks of the Little Avon River in the Cotswolds can now pay £25 to secure thirty-six square feet of woodland on which to spread out the contents of their hamper. Just picnicking amongst your own local habitat will open your eyes to the variety of wildlife; that's a good step along the way to making sure that its value is retained in the community.

Action station

- Aim to minimize your eating out as much as possible. Instead encourage and develop friendships by opening your home or visiting others to eat.
- Next time you stop for a coffee when you're out, make a point of chatting to the people with whom you share your table.

- Try and avoid eating houses where everything your food comes on is throw-away. Venture into the old style caffs which are often cheaper than other places *and* provide you with real cutlery and crockery that is reused again and again.

5
Store Checkout

We live in a consumer culture. Foodwise, we shop to live. But the choices we make about the type of food we buy and where we buy it from have far-reaching consequences for our local community, the environment and people living on the other side of the world. Yet simply because of these consequences of the structure of our economic system, we *can* make positive choices with our purses. We don't have to go along with unjust or criminal practices undertaken by the companies which provide us with food. We can pay our way to change the system by buying foodstuffs that are less damaging, in whatever way, to God's world.

For example, since 1977 there has been united concern about multinational Nestlé's promotion of artificial baby milk across the developing world. In the UK, the campaign group Baby Milk Action (BMAC) suggests that concerned individuals refuse to buy any of the company's brand name goods in protest; one of the most effective ways of making your voice heard by profit-making companies.

For many Christians the idea of boycotting a

product or organization and its produce seems a very negative action. But when the alternative is to support, with the money God has given us, the concerted malnourishment and in my opinion the killing of babies born in the Third World, then it is right to appear negative in a worldly sense. For instead of being encouraged to breast-feed their children – and so help to strengthen an infant's resistance to disease – mothers are supplied with expensive milk powder or solution that must be diluted with the available contaminated water that sickens and even kills. . . .

So it becomes clear that whether you shop in a health food store, corner shop, grocer's or superstore, you can make a difference, whether it's in the actual food you buy or the packaging it's wrapped in. The magazine *Ethical Consumer*, aimed at informing concerned shoppers about the positive choices they can make, in fact lists *twelve* different criteria against which to check the contents of your shopping basket. They include South African connections, support of oppressive regimes, trade union rights, environment, irresponsible marketing, animal testing, factory farming, other animal rights, political donations and registration with the Economic League, a right-wing agency which vets employees for member companies and blacklists those it deems political undesirables. Phew, that's an exhausting and pretty exhaustive list! But amazingly enough there are quite a number of products that are free from any such taint.

God has given us brains to use so that we can make informed decisions about the world around us. Mass communication in the Western world is so vast these days that Christians have no excuse not to be aware and concerned about social issues and how our lives affect the wider world for good *and* bad. Once you start thinking along these lines when it comes to the food you eat or buy, it does get easier, because you naturally start to avoid the destructive stuff on the shop shelves. Of course your choice of food becomes limited, but that is part of the sacrifice of doing things for the Good. And God *will* provide: 'Therefore I tell you, do not worry about your life, what you will eat or drink; or about your body, what you will wear. Is not life more important than food, and the body more important than clothes? Look at the birds of the air; they do not sow or reap or store away in barns, and yet your heavenly Father feeds them. Are you not much more valuable than they? Who of you by worrying can add a single hour to his life?'[1]

It's up to us to make a step of faith and accept that God does supply our needs especially when we are determined to walk His way.

So super?

Because I do most of my shopping in health food stores and greengrocers, I rarely use supermarkets. Some people find that difficult to comprehend. They don't know what they'd do without them. Yet as people become increasingly dependent on supermarkets and the massive out-of-town stores, the selection of thousands of different items people believe they're buying into paradoxically narrows in a very uniform way, and they are trapped in its grip.

One-stop shopping makes us lazy and strangely particular about the food we eat and how it's packaged. A friend of mine complained about the cost of fruit and vegetables. When I replied that in my view greengrocers and market stalls sold some of the cheapest food around, he turned up his nose and declared that food from such places was poor quality.

At the risk of sounding like some female junior Tory health minister – who, if you actually listen to what they're saying talk a lot more common sense than they're given credit for – I have to admit that when people complain that they can't afford such basics as apples, oranges, carrots and potatoes to keep themselves or their families healthy, one has to wonder what food they are buying, how it's packaged and where they're buying it from. I once knew an unemployed woman who did her weekly grocery shopping at Marks & Sparks. And people wonder why they can't make ends meet!

'The market is a façade for the vast amount of middle men who take the grain, fruit, vegetables and meat from the farmer, the wood from the forest, and other raw materials from the primary producers, and process them into finished products.'[2] And it is this processing that we must pay for. There are subtle ways of getting round it. Often 'own brand' products such as cereals and biscuits are made by the same people – and probably on the same conveyor belt – as the more expensive household name brands. Indeed, at one time there was a cross-country chain of supermarkets called International which made a point of selling their products in rather bland blank boxes with nothing but the name of the store and the name of the food it held on the side. They'd now probably be considered very stylish. But the goods *were* very cheap.

Nevertheless, having been brought up on a lot of good, sound Yorkshire home cooking, maybe I'm biased, but I *do* find it quite laughable when a paper such as the *Mirror* homes in on a 'typical weekly shop' by an unemployed person for their family. And lists a jar of coffee, chicken, bacon, Flash, biscuits, bulk crisps, a large can of pilchards, two cans of sardines, a pastry case, two boxes of cereal, a packet of custard mix, four frozen pizzas, four steak and kidney pies, and 4lbs of frozen chips among the items bought.[3]

Let's face it. A lot of that is of the same quality as Mr Ratner's jewellery. I'm not saying that a person on a low income shouldn't buy such items, but all – and more – in a typical week? No wonder in the middle of the 1991 recession, the International Food and Drink Exhibition organizers were able to declare: 'When many industries are facing the toughest year in a decade, food remains the only sector in which consumers are spending more per capita each year and the only one that has consistently shown an upward growth curve year-on-year.'[4] Whatever happened to Home Economics?

The awful thing is that we've let ourselves

become so reliant on supermarkets that we're addicted to the convenience they sell. There are children growing up today in families where a meal is never cooked (in the true sense of the word). For many, to 'have arrived' would be to be able to afford M & S 'throw it in the oven' meals (the irony here is that those who *can* afford them dread going to dinner parties and being presented with a plate of the stuff . . .). Everything comes out of a packet. But if there's a recession and the breadwinner loses their job, the standard of living and in particular the health of the family plummets, simply because they just aren't aware of any other way to supply themselves with food beyond the supermarket shelves. In our society if we suddenly lose our wealth, we have so far to fall.

Some stores like Tesco are doing their bit to redress the balance. They provide plenty of free leaflets concerning health and fitness and 'Green' shopping which at a basic level are very helpful.[5] Pick these up and read them to see how you can adapt your shopping and make it far more healthy and economic. Many companies are making a determined effort to go in the same direction, aware that such changes are welcomed by us consumers: 'In 1990, UK consumers had a purchasing power of £340bn, and with the growth in individual spending power has come the rise, not only of green, but also of ethical, consumerism. We are experiencing a demand for corporate decisions that demonstrate social policies. . . . Operating ethically does not mean operating unprofitably; many of the companies who have strong policies on corporate responsibility also have a good profit and growth record.'[6]

It's certainly a step in the right direction. It is our Christian duty to be ethical consumers; that should go without saying. The fact that food manufacturers, supermarkets and the general public at large are waking up to the impact of our shopping habits is a welcome change that treats God's world and the people on it with a certain respect.

Yet I'm afraid that however hard they try to improve their image, supermarkets *still* bring out the worst in me, and I imagine a great deal of others too. Caught in the midst of harassed mums, bawling kids, uncontrollable trolleys that barricade you in *and* snag your tights as you try to push through in a cramped and confusing superstore, makes me seethe! Or otherwise I'm in the mood to smirk at the absurdity of it all; the wall-to-wall cheeses, the ludicrous amount of choice, and how people take shopping so seriously. God opens my eyes to this strange world around me so that I can laugh at it and see with His eyes the humour of the peculiar games that people play.

When I visit supermarkets I know exactly what I want. I'm usually after a pretty basic thing that the health food store just doesn't sell. Funnily enough it's often something terribly ordinary like bicarbonate of soda. So supermarkets are just not designed for people like me. The powers that be don't want definition. They want spontaneity, people who pick up a tin on a whim. It's very easy to do, but if you're budgeting, take a list of exactly what you want and stick religiously to it. Be careful too of so-called budget vouchers you cut out of magazines or which are slipped through your door. Although they do introduce you to new products and are useful if you're in the mood for a treat, they don't actually save you money unless you already buy the product. Otherwise they tempt you into buying food you wouldn't have considered putting in your shopping basket.

I wander round supermarkets fazed by it all. I look at the rows and stacks and think, 'Crumbs, you need a degree in librarianship to find what you want.' Heck, I have got a degree in librarianship and still I'm confused. Where are you Dewey when we need you? For a classification system, some basic good old-fashioned and *helpful* sign-posting – maybe like the old-style ones you sometimes still see, where you press a button so that a trail of lights comes on, showing where you are and where you want to go – would be ideal. But then people wouldn't dawdle so much. They'd head straight for the packets of cereal and bypass the sticky cakes and 'I'll just treat myself' delicacies, and that isn't good business. But shoppers must be getting sick of tramping around unable to find what they want. It brings to mind the elderly shopper who spent three days in an American department store before she could find her way out. . . .

And when you get to the checkout, there are people with credit cards and trolleys piled high with provisions. I always use cash. I've two things I want to buy. I try to be patient. Adrian Plass

has commented that standing in the ten or less
checkout queue really tests how judgemental you
are. You stand there counting how much the
person in front of you has to see if they're trying to
cheat. You start wondering whether six six-packs
counts as six items or thirty-six. The last time I
was in the ten or less cash only queue, the guy in
front had thirteen items. And a credit card. My
mate Claire, whose bathroom is awash with Ecover
and Body Shop products, tells me she studies what
the person in front is buying to gauge how much
of a Green consumer they are!

Customer service

Make a point of being friendly to the checkout
staff you meet, wherever you happen to shop.
Especially on a Saturday they have to put up with
a lot of hassle and grumpiness, prices not being
marked and tills and bar code machines breaking
down. It can all get a bit heated, and after all,
it's not the best job in the world. But many shop
assistants retain a real sense of humour in the
midst of adversity. As a reporter for the newspaper
of USDAW, the shopworkers' union, I attended
their annual conference. One shop assistant delegate told everyone how it was so cold at the supermarket where she worked that she had to wrap
her feet in the company's plastic bags to keep them
warm while she worked. 'That's nothing,' wrily
announced the next delegate at the podium, 'our
boss makes us pay for them!'

　Chat to the assistants and you'll find that they're

often very friendly. After a long slog of a day – with not too good pay – they need cheering up. Recently I've got into the habit of having porridge for breakfast. I popped into the local Gateway and picked up a massive sack ready for cooking. 'I've made sure I've got my oats', I jokingly remarked as my stuff trundled along the conveyor belt, which raised a smile. It works both ways. Walking past Boots one weekday at the height of Turtlemania I fell in love with a furry hot water bottle cover Raphael. I was in a silly mood so went inside the shop to check him out. I was sold and so was he. I took my new green friend to the till. I felt I had to explain myself some way: 'I couldn't resist him', I sheepishly smiled. 'I know what you mean', replied the shopgirl. 'You just empty him out in the morning. He's much less bother than a man!'

You can build up strong relationships with staff in the smaller shops too. When I do my weekly shop at the health food store and greengrocers I see the same faces; I know who the staff are.

When I worked at the Evangelical Alliance there was a deli a few yards up the Kennington Road run by the Baldoes, a Spanish couple. We'd all pop in there to use up our luncheon vouchers – they certainly knew how to make a stilton and salad in a french bread – and chat away. One friend, Susi from Peru, would have long conversations in her native tongue with them and she built up a strong relationship with this gentle couple. So that when they sold the shop to return to their homeland everyone was genuinely sorry to see them go, and we sent cards and Susi gave them a Spanish Bible as a leaving present. And when we were forced into hunting down other places to eat, I found myself strangely choosy about my sources; I couldn't help noticing how thin cucumber slices were and how few were slapped on the sandwiches, and at a shop where the baps were the size of flying saucers I found myself irritated by women who didn't tie their hair back, and was very aware of the fast turnover of staff.

Where small shops can no longer compete with the supermarkets is that they don't have the space to bulk-buy in such quantities or the market to get rid of it, they lose trade to the larger stores, and so must raise their prices to pay the bills – which turns more shoppers away. And again it's us who ultimately lose out, particularly at a social and community level. We miss the friendly flavour of the local store where the shopkeeper knew your name. It's no accident that there are foods such as crisps, nuts and bread, with olde worlde sounding names like Flannigans to give them the aura of being produced in tiny English villages, when in fact they're churned out from faceless manufactories. It's a nostalgia trip.

Good health?

Many Christians are wary of the New Age aura that seems to envelop many health food stores. It's certainly best to be on your guard, and if you get bad vibes about being in such a place then pray and leave. Once, spending a weekend with my sister in Leeds when she was a student there, we popped into a shop from which she wanted to buy some joss sticks. There were astral charts on the walls and I felt a great sense of unease. It didn't help that the guy sitting behind the shop counter that cut the store in half sported a turtle neck sweater, a wig, and a strange pendant around his neck; he looked every part the stereotype Satanist we see on TV. (You might have noticed that on the box, men of evil in the drama programmes such as The Master in *Doctor Who*, always wear turtle neck sweaters. As one TV critic pondered, 'which came first, the megalomania or the sweater?'). Anyway, health food stores can leave some people with the same sense of unease. My friend Francis works part-time in such a store in London's Portobello Road. One Saturday I happened to be visiting the local market, and not having seen him for a while visited him at the shop to catch up on news. I showed him the Green lifestyle book I'd written, and on realizing that it was a Christian book he remarked that it couldn't be stocked in the shop. I turned to look at the books that were on sale and my view was blocked by floor to ceiling carousel displays of books brought out by New Age publishers. That's not to say that all such books are bad. The first, and best, veggie cook book I ever bought was Jan Hunt's *A vegetarian in the family*[7] which is published by Thorsons. But the fact that these books were on sale to the exclusion of any other type of publisher gave some indication of where the store was coming from.

But should we avoid such places on principle? Some Christians will choose not even to lighten their doors. Because I can't get a lot of my food elsewhere, the I'm happy to stick with them. If I were buying into their homeopathic and alternative medicines then there'd be cause for concern. And not just on a spiritual level. It's healthy to question the promotion of so-called 'healthy' supplements. Multivitamins rarely contain more than seven of the thirteen vitamins we daily need to keep us healthy. And according to the Consumers Association, royal jelly contains fewer nutrients than a bowl of cornflakes! So it's back to Kellogg's, Cliff. Indeed, sixty to seventy per cent of this food of queen bees and the Princess of Wales is actually water. Indeed, the last time I was in my local health food store, the manager was telling a new sales assistant this very fact. 'But that sounds like a con', gasped the sceptical rookie. 'That's because it is a con', I muttered loudly as I wandered past, thinking of all the pills and potions on sale that are fobbed off on the customer. I always feel slightly sad when I see elderly people seeking relief from their arthritis or whatever with the store manager acting the medical expert recommending certain products. And I can't help recalling that great Mandy Rice Davis saying, 'He would, wouldn't he?' After all, a shop manager's job is to shift stock. They get commission too on particular brands, so it's in their interest to encourage people to buy certain products.

But though it's easy to get hot under the collar about some of the activities of health food stores, it's important that we similarly consider the chain stores and more mainstream shops in the light of our faith. Is the way they trade, or treat their staff, ideal? How is the shop contributing to the local community? Are its goods fairly priced? Do the goods it sells exploit people or places or the environment and animals, which ultimately all belong to God? Shopping at any type of shop is not an easy option. It's important that as Christians we make it our duty to find out what we're actually buying into through the food we bite into.

Never on a Sunday?

The growing trend towards seven-day shopping may seem a great convenience; the shops are there when you want them. But it isn't just Christians who want to make sure that Sundays keep their distinctive nature while at the same time ironing out the strange discrepancies – such as being able to buy a soft porn magazine but not a Bible on the seventh day.

As a staff reporter on the newspaper of the shop-workers' union USDAW I was very privileged to be working there in April 1986 when in a surprise move the House of Lords voted against full-scale Sunday trading. The next morning at USDAW HQ everybody was walking round with Cheshire Cat grins. For shopworkers and anyone working in trades that feed the shops, such as the distribution industry, had a lot to lose. Yet it was recognized that what at one point was going to be termed 'an unholy alliance' of Church, shopworkers and the Labour movement (until the publicity department decided that perhaps it wasn't the most diplomatic of slogans) was an important unity. Each group could learn from the others in its understanding of the vast array of issues that unrestricted Sunday trading provokes.

Once shops start trading on Sunday it whittles away at the shopworker's right to have a regular day off. And the bonus often paid for working unsociable hours is wiped away as once unsociable hours become seen as normal working hours. This can have a devastating effect on low-income families. It's bad enough that someone has to work on the one day when most families can spend time together, but if the extra pay is cut, then that adds insult to injury and causes great hardship. Not only that, but other workers will lose their freedom too. Once people make a habit of buying their food and whatever on Sundays, then service industries must shake into action to serve those people; eating places, police, car park attendants et al. It'll be just another day for these people too.

But that's not how God meant it to be: 'And God blessed the seventh day and made it holy, because on it He rested from all the work of creating that He had done.'[8] For the Jews, their seventh or Sabbath day is Saturday. Christians in remembrance of Jesus' resurrection place more importance on Sunday. And as a lot of Jewish laws regarding cooking and the use of utensils are not only believed to be spiritually beneficial, but are also instruction for ensuring physical cleanliness, so having one day off in seven is as much a physical pick-you-up as a spiritual one.

Try to avoid buying food on Sunday, and having

lunchtime pub meals instead of the traditional Sunday dinner at home. Bar staff along with newsagents tend to be forgotten when the issue of Sunday work is broached, but they've rarely had any real choice about their rest days. Be very wary of any shop that goes on about the freedom of Sunday trading; the only freedom they're interested in is the freedom to make as much money as possible. Yet there's a strange logic in all this: we only have a limited amount of money to spend, and most of us have enough trouble making it last six days. Not only that, but it's costly to open on Sundays; staff have to be paid the extra day, the bills stretch higher, and shop prices increase accordingly so that the profit margin isn't squeezed. And that's *all* prices, whatever day you do your shopping. I'm intrigued, I must admit, by the legal implications of shoplifting on a Sunday. If a supermarket breaks the law by Sunday trading then they can hardly argue against any criminal tendencies their customers might have on that day!

The arrival of the European market should clarify the laws for everyone. In fact, many EC countries are stricter than we are, so our quiet Sundays may remain after all.

Action station

- Read:
  The Green Consumer Guide by John Elkington and Julia Hailes (Victor Gollancz 1988)
  Born to Shop by Mike Starkey (Monarch 1989)

Superfoods by Barbara Griggs and Michael van
   Stratten (Dorling Kindersley 1991)

- Subscribe to the *Ethical Consumer*. Write to
  ECRA Publishing Ltd, 100 Gretney Walk, Moss
  Side, Manchester M15 5ND for further details.

- Aim to buy food that is wrapped in as little
  packaging as possible. Choose cardboard boxes
  or glass jars and bottles rather than types of
  plastics, and take the empties to recycling centres. Carry a carrier bag with you when you go
  shopping so that you don't have to buy, and
  waste, another.

- For further information about Baby Milk
  Action's Nestlé boycott, write to BMAC, 6
  Regent Terrace, Cambridge CB2 1AA.

- For further information about the Keep Sunday
  Special Campaign, write to KSS, Jubilee
  House, 3 Hooper Street, Cambridge CB1 2NZ

6
From the Freezer to the Microwave

Our hi-tech world has got the better of us. Instead of it serving us, we seem to have lost some of our humanity through the way we use it. In the kitchen, so-called mod cons (which the cynic might argue are exactly what they say they are) designed to reduce household drudgery in reality tie women in particular to the home. In the same way that the car proved such a success story that it jammed the roads, so that in city streets it's turned out to be no faster on average than a horse-drawn vehicle at the turn of the century (about 8 mph), so people who use many kitchen gadgets – food processors, blenders and choppers – find that they spend as much if not more time cleaning the wretched things than the job would have taken had they used a simple kitchen knife.

In our high-speed lives where real home cooking is becoming as much a hobby as, say, dress-making (another activity which was once just as much a necessity), people resort to pre-packaged foods that are ready in minutes. Glossy adverts promise days of idle leisure without hours spent in the kitchen, which may to an extent be true, but the *quality* of food has been dropped and replaced by the uniform and oh-so-familiar flavours of ready-to-eats. Such packaged meals are certainly not cheap either.

As we rush headlong into the twenty-first century, we appear desperate to throw off ordinary living and be transported into a sci-fi world where delicious foods are quick-cook and streamlined. But in this tightening of what food is all about, we lose a lot of the basic enjoyment of eating together, and the basic pleasure of preparing a meal. 'The pleasure of cookery is not confined to eating the finished product. Most food is relaxing and deeply satisfying to prepare. Choosing, feeling and smelling the raw produce is an integral part of the cooking process, just as choosing, following and possibly departing from a recipe. Buying ready-made food diminishes those pleasures.'[1] Home cooking is a feast for the senses.

Don't get me wrong, I fully realize that home cooking *is* time-consuming, and unfortunately many people in our high-speed culture just don't have the time. But it's certainly their loss. Proper cooking *is* a creative process, and as such we put a lot of love and care into what we make. I recall once reading about a young mentally retarded girl who had a cooking lesson alongside more able children. She got covered in flour and pastry, and her scones didn't turn out perfect and hardly matched the quality of her schoolmates', but her own delight in what she'd made and baked and the love that was folded with the other ingredients into her mixture made those scones very special to her mother.

Out of a tin

Certainly canned food is useful at times. If guests turn up unannounced and you need to rustle up a quick meal at very short notice, then they're your lifeline. They last for ages unopened so it's wise to keep a few in your food cupboard in case of emergencies. It's a useful skill to be able to disguise a tinned soup. Add herbs, some grated cheese, and a few fine slices from whatever vegetable – or fruit – you happen to have handy, and hey presto, you've an exotic new brand!

But be careful not to become too dependent on getting everything out of a tin. You'll be missing out on so much. When I had Domestic Science lessons at school I would spend ages chopping up Bramleys and various veg, while getting more and more irritated that I was the one in the class who had to have a mother who sent me to school with the uncut version because she was loathe to heed the teacher's instruction to buy a tin of fruit or veg! Which of course all the other mothers had duly done. Yet Mum and I laugh about it now. And I know that were I in a similar position I'd probably do exactly the same to my own child. I'm honestly glad that my ma made a point of emphasizing what home cooking was all about.

No wonder the lesson was called Domestic Science and not Home Economics. For getting food out of a can is hardly economic. And when I've been on the dole, I've valued even more what my mum was saying through her action – and through her continued home cooking. While my school teacher was implying that tinned food was convenient, she was inadvertently suggesting that preparing a meal from scratch was a thing of the past and not worth the effort. And this was to the supposedly brighter Grammar school girls, so I dread to think what the Secondary Modern lot were being taught. Though from the dark recesses of my mind I seem to remember that while we were exploding baked apples in the ovens during our first lesson, they were learning the wonders of concocting Welsh Rarebit and a cup of tea. . . .

Still, on that score I can't complain. The best introduction to cooking I've ever come across is *Observer* journalist Katharine Whitehorn giving the recipe for a boiled egg in her cookery book aimed at people living in bedsits. Don't laugh, not everybody knows, and so it was very wise and clearsighted of her to include it. Not knowing such a simple practice is not something you want to admit to. (Put an egg in a pan of water, add a pinch of salt to the water, and heat until the water boils. Some reckon that if you turn the heat off at this point, thus saving energy and leave the egg in the slowly cooling water, the egg will be ready in about the same time as if you'd left the water boiling away. I seem to have more success when keeping the heat on. Though one time I got so engrossed in the paper I was reading at the breakfast table that I clean forgot my egg until there was a loud explosion and bits of egg flew across the kitchen. In normal circumstances a boiled egg should be ready in two or three minutes.)

At a basic financial level, making your own meals is far more rewarding. An article in the *Observer* reported on young home owners pressured by high interest rates on their mortgages to the extent that they were finding it practically impossible to make ends meet. A member of one pair stated that when times seemed *really* tough she would take the advice of her grandmother and buy herself a potato, a carrot and an onion; 'With those you have a soup' her granny would say. And it was a recipe I regularly clung onto when I spent five months in early 1991 living in London on £22 a week social security. You can keep a good soup going for days just by topping it up with water and fresh ingredients. I became an expert at making my own bread too. Which opened my eyes to gems of wisdom that gleamed within Jesus' parables: 'The kingdom of heaven is like yeast that a woman took and mixed into a large amount of flour until it worked all through the dough.'[2]

Package deal

When we pass along the supermarket shelves we need to consider not only the food we're about to buy, but what it's wrapped in. The world has limited resources and it is therefore important that they're not squandered on wasteful packaging. The modern world has thrown up a mass of interesting forms of wrapping way beyond the tried and tested card and glass, the basic containers of yesteryear.

Of course, food does need to be covered to keep it uncontaminated. The surest way to be put off an iced bun sitting in a bakery window is to spot a wasp or bluebottle wading across the snowy white topping. While many food producers *are* switching to 'environmentally sound' containers in a bid to satisfy the Green consumer, they unfortunately don't suit their purpose all the time. One wholefood company which a few years ago packed its crunchy cereal in biodegradeable plastic bags found the plastic wasn't stable enough and that the bags began to deteriorate on the store shelves if they sat there too long. The company soon had to resort to ordinary and environmentally unsound placcy bags instead.

A minimum amount of packaging is necessary to satisfy health and safety regulations and ensure that food stays fresh, but we seem to have gone to the other extreme. Off the top of my head I can immediately think of a certain brand of exceedingly good apple pies which sit in little silver foil dishes and are packaged six to a cardboard box in a moulded plastic bright red tray. An awful lot of money from our pockets goes towards paying for such packaging excesses. One shop I came across in Yorkshire, specializing in selling nuts, dried fruit and cereals by the scoop-load out of great big barrels, had a notice in its window claiming that for every £30 spent on foodstuffs from supermarkets and the like, £5 goes on the packaging! When you go shopping for food, do consider the outer

coating as much as the food within. God not only
wants us to be good stewards of His creation,
but of the money He's provided us with too. It's
important that we make sure that we're not throwing our money away on worthless wrapping.

A lot of people still throw away recycleable
materials such as glass, paper, card and plastic
bags, as well as aluminium cans and foil, despite
recent emphasis on being more Green. Since the
world has a limited supply of raw materials it is
vital that we in the West in particular (since we
are the main consumers of the world's resources),
make a point of checking out where our goods and
the packaging that surrounds them actually come
from, and where they ultimately go.

'We all produce household waste, and most of
this is buried on land. About half this waste could
be usefully recycled . . . Producing an aluminium
can from recycled material takes one twentieth of
the energy needed to produce a can from raw
materials.'[3]

If you're going to buy a chocolate bar, for example, avoid those wrappers that simply are screwed
up and thrown in the bin because there's nothing
else you can do with them. Turn instead to the
old-fashioned style wrapped ones in aluminium
foil with a paper label. You can take the foil to
Oxfam or Guide Dogs for the Blind, and I use the
underside of the labels to write my shopping list
on or as labels for reusing envelopes. On any food
you buy, aim to avoid composite wrappers, that is
packaging that does the job but uses a variety of
materials such as card, plastics, polystyrene or foil.

Not only are such wrappers expensive but they are practically impossible to recycle. Go instead for simple packaging that does the job and nothing more. Be wary of being taken in by the gloss or status of the label on the packet. Many 'own brand' products come off exactly the same conveyor belt as the more upmarket name brands and are a fraction of the price because they are a very basic design and formula. And ponder on the fact that while it may appear that we have a seemingly unlimited and mindblowing amount of choice on our shop shelves, in reality only about five companies actually produce the food we buy.

For fruit and vegetables God has already provided wrappers and you shouldn't need another. Politely decline any bag that's offered, and always take a carrier bag with you when you go shopping so you won't need to ask – or pay – for another.

Freeze frame

An indication of how much frozen food has taken a hold on us is that a staggering ninety-eight per cent of us eat frozen foods. What that figure *actually* means I'm not at all sure. Apart from a rare bag of peas or veggy cocktail sausages I never buy frozen food; I can quite happily live without a freezer cabinet.

Certainly these days many people regularly dip into their local store's freezer for something exotically ordinary for their tea. But like any technological development Christians need to question their dependency on it. We all know of people who stock up on hunks of meat and ice cream as if they're getting ready for a siege. (Personally I'm of the theory that if civilization were to break down, it would be the vegetarians who would last out. Their jars of beans and lentils could well outlast food that needs an electricity supply to keep it fresh . . .) But then, maybe we shouldn't be questioning what people put in their fridges, so much as the need people feel for greed.

Certainly freezers are really useful when preparing for a large party or, say, church bazaar. The Church of England's Children's Society holds an annual Great Cake Bake, and to prepare for this local Christians can have an 'all hands on deck' cooking session and make use of any freezers available to them to keep cakes fresh until they're sold to raise funds. But apart from this, there seems something strange about filling up what is basically a trunk large enough to hold a couple of stacked human bodies just for the sake of it.

Still, since pantries became very much a thing of the past, we've needed a place where basics like milk, butter and leftover morsels can stay cool and fresh. In the developed world we're very fortunate. One very distinct sign of our standing is that we have ice at our disposal during hot weather. We can produce and store it easily whatever the climate.

In the movie *Mosquito Coast*, based on Paul Theroux's novel, Harrison Ford as the main character goes native with his family in Belize, but in doing so plans also to show the locals what the so-called civilized world has to offer. He builds an ice-making machine and ultimately brings the people and their lush environment into contact with the worst excesses of the developed world. The film includes a memorable scene where Ford wraps a slab of ice in a damp cloth and treks through the harsh jungle and up a steep hill to a group of tribespeople, with the intention of showing them what he has on offer. By the time he reaches his destination the ice block has melted and the water seeps through the cloth and between his fingers.

Ice *is* a luxury and we are very fortunate that we are able to freeze our foods and extend their life. But be careful to check how long food can be kept cold, and, indeed, whether it's healthy for it to be stored in the freezer at all. Milk, cheese, eggs and cooked fish are among foodstuffs that one shouldn't freeze, but other foods *do* have a rec-ommended time limit in both fridge and freezer. Be sure to label products with the date you first put them in the freezer, for safety's sake. While restaurant refrigerators have to conform to strict health standards, in the home we tend to be more lax, which in the case of meat and dairy products in particular can prove very dangerous. Not only that, but food that is 'off' and is sitting in the fridge or freezer has a knock-on effect on the freshness of other foods. Be sure then to read the freezing instructions on the side of each packet of food and follow accordingly.

It's also important that anyone getting rid of an old fridge or freezer be very careful where they dispose of it. Large self-locking tomb-shaped freez-ers can be exactly that if children climb inside them. In an environmental sense too, fridges and freezers release harmful CFCs that damage the ozone layer and so ultimately life on earth. Contact your local council to find out where you can properly dispose of your fridge. For we need to be careful that the pressures of our society which tempt us to amass and amass don't tempt us into over-indulgence of this good gift which God has provided us with.

Microwaving, not dining?

If you've ever seen the movie *Rain Man* you'll know there's a terrifying scene where Dustin Hoffman as the autistic Raymond accidentally leaves the door to the microwave open while he's cooking some food. The smoke that begins to spew out sets off the fire alarm. A distraught Raymond is frighteningly disorientated until his brother (Tom Cruise) calms him down.

A not too dissimilar thing happened to me when I was living in a rented house in Kingston. I'd decided to make some toast but the toaster was broken and there was no grill on the oven. Instead I placed the slice of bread in the microwave, clicked the door shut and set the timer. I'd done this before, and though the bread would come out a strangely damp but hard consistency it was recognizable as toast.

This time something went horribly wrong. Thick black smoke began seeping out of the sides of the oven door filling the kitchen and dining room as well as my lungs. I broke outside into the cold night and gulped cool air as my eyes watered and I coughed up the smoke. Never have I been so thankful to breathe in London air. It was a frightening experience. I could see the headlines: 'Killed by a piece of toast.' It would rival the *South London Press*'s 'Goldfish dies of cocaine overdose' headline classic. The microwave bell pinged and I pulled out the charred remains of my piece of bread.

Microwave food doesn't have to be such a nightmare experience. Indeed, these days the ovens are commonplace in homes, cafés and restaurants across the land. They are quick and convenient, particularly if unexpected guests arrive or you've had a hard day and all you're in the mood for is throwing something in the 'box' which will be ready in five minutes.

Yet we need to proceed with caution. Part of being a Christian is surely about being prepared to question things and not necessarily accept what we're being told – or sold – at face value. Certainly we should be trusting but that doesn't mean being gullible. For many people, microwaves *do* have an important role to play. They take up little space and so are increasingly considered as ideal for bedsits and college rooms, and general quick and easy living. People who are sick or elderly find that the time and energy saved through using a microwave can be a real boon. For homeless people forced to stay in bed and breakfast hotels instead of proper council accommodation, a microwave saves space and in theory serves them better than dangerously cooking on the floor, as some people must do.

Yet ironically it is to vulnerable and sick people that microwaves can be most dangerous. In late 1989 it was discovered that an incredible one in three microwave ovens failed to heat food thoroughly to seventy degrees centigrade. And somehow such a dreadful statistic got pushed under the carpet and had little effect on sales. Anybody who has ever eaten microwaved food has at some point bitten into supposedly 'cooked food' that turned out to be lukewarm or actually still cold.

When travelling it is important to be wary of food that has been cooked, allowed to cool and then reheated as required. Such food is an ideal breeding ground for bacteria. 'Inside the glamorous carton is a high-risk food item, and my advice is to avoid such products on the grounds of poor quality, uncertain nutrition and possible bacterial contamination', warns Dr Richard Lacey.[4]

Any bacteria that are killed off in the reheating process are on the surface, but we all know as Christians that it's the inside which matters. It can only be a matter of time before someone dies from salmonella or some other kind of poisoning which a microwave oven failed to kill off. Used for thawing food, they can't be guaranteed to heat the food through completely either.

When you're storing food, be careful to avoid using cling film at all costs. There was actually a time on earth when people managed to live without wrapping food up in the stuff. They used old fashioned implements such as jars, pots and bowls with a plate put on top! I never buy cling film or rolls of aluminium foil. Both are totally unnecessary. If I have to wrap up sandwiches I put them in a paper bag rather than cover them in a sheet of metal. Cling film is particularly dangerous when food is hot. Chemicals from the plastic can leach out and contaminate food. It certainly doesn't mix well with microwaves.

People depend on their new ovens, some to the extent that they don't bother cooking any other way. Certainly microwaves are good for reheating recently cooked meals, and in particular for baking spuds as they're cooked so quickly. Mind you, if that's your main reason for considering getting one, you might as well go and pay the exorbitant one-quid-plus a spud, at the local Spud U Like, and let the people there bother about the preparation and washing up instead!

Personally I'm of the persuasion that when it comes to safety, one of the most important experiments that needs to be done on any new invention is the test of time. In the same way that I wouldn't wear contact lenses because I can just imagine in twenty years those people who've worn them for so long wandering around as if they're extras from the film *The Day of the Triffids*, I'm wary of what could happen to those who rely in microwave ovens to the same extent.

Action station

- Read:
  Safe shopping, safe cooking, safe eating by Dr Richard Lacey (Penguin 1989)

- Aim to reduce your reliance on microwaved or frozen food. If you have a glut of food such as blackberries, consider making jam, wine or bottling them for future use instead.

- When you next go shopping look for a cheaper alternative to over-packed and over-priced frozen foods.

- Always follow the instructions on the side of the packet regarding freezing and cooking food. Follow the instructions too for looking after your freezer and microwave to ensure that they work at their most efficient.

- If you know a sick or elderly person, bake them some food in a proper oven for friendship's sake *and* to prevent microwave cooking affecting their health while they're at an already low ebb.

7
Growing Your Own

We've got so used to getting everything – beans, fruit salad, soups and even spuds – out of a tin or a packet these days, that the very idea of cultivating a patch of land, particularly for people in the cities, seems very pre-Industrial Revolution.

Yet God has provided for all our needs in a very natural way. We *can* grow our own food, and technically even harvest and produce our own clothes, but God's provision isn't necessarily a call to the Good Life. Indeed, in the UK where so much of the land is privately owned, it's very difficult for individuals who've fallen on hard times or just want a change of scene, to live legally off the land. Unlike places such as the US and the Scandinavian countries, it's practically impossible over here to find a spare patch of land where we can carve out a plot and build a home if we've grown too tired of urban living.

Nevertheless, we should bear in mind that there are plenty of foodstuffs literally growing on trees. And we should open our eyes to the fact that God has made sure we've had all we need for living ever since the beginning of time.

But even then it wasn't quite there for the taking. It was our job to prune and cultivate so that nature could reach its full potential in God's sight. 'The Lord God took the man and put him in the Garden of Eden to work it and take care of it.'[1]

That truth remains the same today, even though it's tougher this time round. God's provision remains the same, but growing our own just became a more difficult, back-breaking task. Weeds and pests now suffocate and wear away at food-bearing plants, soil has toughened, and bad weather takes its toll on crops and those who farm them. It's certainly not an easy option. 'Cursed is the ground because of you, through painful toil you will eat of it all the days of your life. It will produce thorns and thistles for you, and you will eat the plants of the field. By the sweat of your brow you will eat your food until you return to the ground since from it you were taken, for dust you are and to dust you will return.[2] Phew!

But don't be put off. The perseverance pays off. The great thing about growing food as opposed to just plants is that there's something to eat at the end of it! It always amazes me that people growing sunflowers aren't tempted to cut the flowers off in their prime for a tasty snack! Certainly sunflowers bring a zany brightness to any garden, and maybe I've been in too many health food stores, but I can't view one without thinking of nibbling the seeds!

Free for all?

I can quite understand Jesus and His disciples munching their way among the corn.[3] Sure it was on the Sabbath, which didn't please the legalistic Pharisees too much, but by His actions Jesus was not only saying that it's OK to eat if you're hungry on your day of rest, but also that God satisfies people at their point of need. And by the way, Jesus isn't giving the go-ahead for a bit of scrumping either! In those days, farmers left part of their crop at the edge of the field for the poor – a great idea God wrote into the Old Testament to make sure people didn't go hungry. It's a pity we still don't do that today. The nearest we get is probably eat-as-much-as-you-like strawberry picking, which stretches to the more exotic oranges or olives the further afield in Europe you go.

Nevertheless there are still rich pickings to be had. When we view the world as God's world, we have our eyes opened to what He's made available. It's refreshing when out for a stroll to come across a bramble bush and be able to satisfy any slight hunger pangs immediately. Or if you happen to know a patch where fruit is growing wild, have a picking session with friends, and either store the fruit for a later date or make a quick crumble, pie or a delicious summer pudding when you get home, and share it among the workers. It certainly makes up for all the stained fingers and scratched hands! If you've space for all the paraphernalia that brewing requires, why not make your own fruity wine? Not into alcohol?

Then make a real fruity drink instead by boiling up your fruit in some water, sieving the juice into a jug and put this in the fridge to cool. Don't throw the remaining mulch away, but add a dollop of yoghurt for a simple yet very refreshing pudding.

And don't be put off foraging if you live in a built-up area. When I worked at Tear Fund in Teddington – which is a sort of build-up area – I would pass the local police station every morning on my way to the office. There was a pear tree laden with juicy ripe fruit on a patch of grass next to the station, and whenever I passed it I always thought that if I were a police officer I'd get a ladder out and shin up the tree. . . . One morning the tree was full of cackling birds having a whale of a time feasting on the fruit. Pears that had fallen were lying ready to rot in the grass. It seemed such a waste. But though I'm a shy girl at heart, I'd just been to see the movie *Dead Poets' Society* so I told myself 'C'mon Catherine, seize the day', and boldly asked the officer at reception if it was OK (which was probably the strangest request he'd had all day), and duly hopped over the wall and collected all the pears within reach.

Even more bizarre, one day I was shopping in Kingston and was wandering along by the fruit and veg stalls when I came across a huge potato sitting in the middle of the pavement. 'Hello, potato, what are you doing there?' I asked. (I didn't actually.) But there were lots of people walking around it and saying observant things like 'There's a potato'. It was obviously there for a reason, so I picked it up, took it home, dusted it off and had a lovely baked spud!

On my bike I've had to screech to a halt a couple of times for the same reason. I have this theory that if people drop their shopping bags or they split, the loose fruit and veg rolls off the pavement into the kerb and people don't like picking stuff up off the ground. It doesn't bother me. Heck, it's been buried in mud for so many months, had earthworms crawl around it or been out in all weathers, and, if you're especially unlucky, been waxed and irradiated too, that a little bit of grime's not going to make much difference. It just needs a good wash.

A lot of my pride was washed off when I was touring Norway. When I arrived I saw tramps looking for deposit bottles in the bins at Oslo Railway Station. I remember thinking that must be pretty desperate. But the country was so expensive that by the end of my stay I wasn't quite rifling through bins for glass, but I was on the look-out.

Back in England it took me a few months before I could look at a Coke bottle without thinking 'one kroner' (about ten pence). One scorching hot day, sitting parched in an Oslo park, I said to God, 'I could really do with a drink, but I can't afford one Lord. Could I have one, please?' A short while later I found an empty bottle by the side of the road. Added to the small change I already had I was able to buy a small ice lolly and still be left with a couple of pfennigs to tip the shop assistant. No, I didn't.

In such dire straits you do become more aware

of the amount of wasted food there is; of food left at the side of a plate or drinks left half-drunk. When I hear of children brought up to 'leave some for Mr Manners' as a show of politeness, I can't help thinking that that's exactly what it is; a public show. Fair enough if somebody genuinely can't finish what's on their plate, but to leave food for the sake of leaving food when there are millions of hungry people in the world, as well as the immediate people who've taken the trouble to prepare a meal, strikes me as an absolute insult, and pure bad manners.

Restaurants and bakeries are notorious for getting rid of their perishable food at the end of the day. Indeed, when I was in Manchester there was a chain of cheap bakeries that made a killing out of slightly stale bread and buns. . . . Once in Paris and coming face-to-face with a genuine Parisian patisserie, I was stunned into wondering 'Who eats all these cakes?' I just couldn't comprehend how so many similar shops, selling such exotic and rich food every day, could exist. I'm told that at the end of the day they sell off cheaply any remaining ones.

Tending the garden

But generally you shouldn't have to resort to desperate foraging measures, though they're useful to bear in mind when times are hard. God has made us creative beings with a responsibility to look after His world. We can combine the two *and* get a meal out of it by cultivating a patch of land. You might

be fortunate to have a garden available to you, or
if you live in a pokey bedsit the best you can do
might be growing a batch of cress on an old flan-
nel. Either way, the watering, nurturing and
simple watching and waiting can be a very touching act.

'Someone, aware of what people lack when they
live cocooned urban lives, recommended growing
lettuce seed in a bowl. Watching the plantlets
develop is an activity somehow conducive to
health and wholeness. In a miniscule way the
grower becomes aware of the conditions of growth
which are good for him as well as the lettuce . . .
The natural world should play an essential part in
our daily lives and in our spiritual awareness.'[4]

Instead of talking to the plants, talk to God while
you're caring for this new life; your crop will benefit anyway from all that carbon dioxide you're
breathing out while you're doing it. And spiritually there's a lot to be learnt from tending a crop.
We begin to understand how God strengthens and
cultivates and prunes us too. We see the need for
outside help. 'I am the true vine, and my Father
is the gardener', taught Jesus. 'He cuts off every
branch in me that bears no fruit, while every
branch that does bear fruit He trims clean so that
it will be even more fruitful.'[5] By looking after our
own patch we're developing a clearer picture of
the necessity of direction, discipline and devotion
that, yes, a plant needs, to grow strong, but that
we ourselves need if we are to grow and remain
strong in our Christian faith.

I'm always slightly bemused – and saddened –

when I see people have concreted over their gardens. Obviously they have the right to do what they want with their own patch. But it does seem a shame. It says something about the owner, but I'm not altogether sure what. Something terribly soulless, I fear. My parents' next-door neighbours have erected an eight foot high wooden fence all around their back garden. It's like Fort Knox. That's a bit easier to read. It says something along the lines, of 'We don't really want to know the people who live at the back and on either side of us'. . . . Many people in the UK are fortunate to have a space to call their own, and growing their own food with some flowers and a lawn for leisure is a way of balancing the home budget.

If you have access to a garden, do aim to cultivate a part of it. Occasionally it's nice to see space run wild, but our role as Christians is at least to pray for it if not tidy it up a bit. Getting some food out of it is an added bonus. If you're renting, it's easy to get into the 'it's not worth the effort, I might not be here in a year's time' syndrome. When you're planning to grow food you may well not see the finished product until the following year. But is that any reason not to bother to plant at all?

The tenants who follow would very likely be pleased to know that you made the effort in order that they've got fresh fruit and vegetables just outside their home. My mate Helen moved on from having got into gardening at her previous rent. She tells me that she had to resist the temptation to nip back in the middle of the night and reap the harvest!

In some ways, it's as with our Christian faith. God puts us in a particular place or with a particular person and we do our bit in His name, not knowing the outcome before we've moved on to another situation. We've done our bit in the chain. When you move home often, you can either tell yourself it's not worth putting time and energy into self-sacrificing activities, or you can say, 'I can only do what I can do for God and it's up to Him to do what He will,' and hand the bat to the next player after you've reached your furthest base.

It reminds me of the time I stayed for a week with my sister Jane in her shared flat in London's Notting Hill Gate while I was searching for accommodation, having recently got a job in SW London. She wasn't getting on too well with her flatmates, and while this was reaching its climax I was visiting a landlord to look at a room. En route I'd picked a batch of brambles and returned to my sis's intent on concocting a summer pudding. It was sitting cooling in the fridge when my sister had her final 'that's it' argument with the self-appointed Queen Bee of the flat, and Jane and I both ended up out on the streets. As I helped her lug assorted tapes, rucksack and duvet round to her friend's, I couldn't help thinking of the summer pudding sitting in the fridge. Before we'd left I'd told one of the other tenants that she could have it for her tea. She was Peruvian and I doubted that she had tasted this British delicacy before. I pictured her enjoying it.

Ripe, strawberries, ripe

We may moan about our inclement weather, but it is ideal for growing your own produce. Of course crops will occasionally fail, blights will attack the budding fruits and the damp could rot your plants, but you'll also be surprised at how much your land will produce. If you live with your parents, you may already eat of the fruit of their land. Take responsibility for a small corner of the garden and see what you can encourage to grow.

Take a few tips from the Bible. The parables, for example, have as much to teach us about basic farming techniques as about our walk with God. When Jesus told the parable of the sower, he homed in on the interest of his rural listeners and took them all a step further. With so many city dwellers in the UK God uses this passage as a gardening, farming guide as well as teaching us about our receptiveness to Him.

'Then he told them many things in parables, saying: "A farmer went out to sow his seed. As he was scattering the seed . . . some fell on rocky places, where it did not have much soil. It sprang up quickly, because the soil was shallow. But when the sun came up, the plants were scorched and they withered because they had no root. Other seed fell among thorns, which grew up and choked the plants. Still other seed fell on good soil, where it produced a crop – a hundred, sixty or thirty times what was sown." '[6]

That's basic good sense, and as much a call to care for the soil itself as for the seedlings we plant.

For soil is literally the foundation for life on the earth's surface. Good soil contains the nutrients that plants need to flourish, on which animals and humans can feed. But it is the plant roots and covering that knit the earth together. That is part of God's great balancing act. Upset it and life dries up. In poor parts of the world, people resort to chopping down trees for firewood and homes, and food for their livestock in order to live, but leave desert plains in their wake. In the middle of the USA wheat farms have turned to dust bowls, and in Central American rain forests barren land is all that remains in some parts, now that beef cattle reared for burgers have laid waste the ground where towering hardwoods once stood and exotic creatures swarmed.

In the Old Testament the Israelites honoured God by giving the first fruits of their crop to the priests – which kept the priests healthy too. I'm sure your minister would be very grateful if you gave him a batch of your new carrots, but in general the nearest we seem to get to that law these days is at Harvest Festival, where members of the congregation leave a tin of beans on the altar steps halfway through the service for later delivery to the local hospital or old people's home.

But it doesn't have to be that way. 'Honour the Lord with your wealth, with the first fruits of all your crops; then your barns will be filled to overflowing, and your vats will brim over with new wine.'[7] Ask God to help you to honour Him with your crops. Share with your neighbours. Cook a casserole or pie and take it round to an elderly person who lives on their own. Give a bunch of fruit to the beggar on the street. Use your fruit and veg to put love into action.

By their very presence your plants will enrich the local environment too. Some plants such as herbs are not only useful for cooking, but add flavour to their surroundings, as well as looking attractive. On other plants it's the fruit itself that brings colour, such as cherries and strawberries. I'm struck by the 'colour' brought by the rich variety of stuff my parents have grown in an ordinary suburban garden over the years. Apples, gooseberries, blackberries, red currants, tomatoes, pears, rhubarb, peas, strawberries, raspberries, the odd peach, a clump of potatoes, marrows, runner beans, cabbages and cherries. . . . It's about having strawberries on your morning bowl of cornflakes, blackberry jam, and playing Tinker, Tailor with your cherry stones and finding you've far, far more stones than occupations. . . .

Growing food locally is also very important for keeping strains of fruit and vegetables going. The English apple industry was decimated when we joined the Common Market. If we haven't been much good at anything else, at least we could grow apples. But the range was all but replaced by the tart Granny Smiths – true they're delicious, but they left a bad taste in the mouth because they were South African and buying them was a vote for the apartheid system; French Golden Delicious, the promoter of which should have been done under the Trade Descriptions Act; and English Coxes. And, yes, they do taste good, in a nice sort of way, and they rattle when you shake them, but there's far more to our apples than that. Across the country there remain apple connoisseurs, as there are Real-Alers, who go in search of elusive brands.

It's important to support farmers who still cultivate the fine strains of apples. Indeed, there's an organization called the Brogdale Trust which deals in this very area. Brogdale Orchards in Kent are devoted to preserving all the rich variety of English apples that still exist. If we were to lose any of these strains, it would be a very sad thing for our rural heritage.

Who knows, the apple tree at the bottom of your garden may produce an unusual type. Or maybe the apples just taste interestingly different to the ones you buy in the shops. They come in all shapes and sizes too, which isn't what you can say about the cling-filmed, polystyrene trayed, unform four to a pound ones you get at your local supermarket. Personally I can't understand why anyone would want to buy uniform apples. Maybe they're the same people who concrete over their gardens. We should delight in the difference. Certainly God does. After all, He made you and me. And He made little green apples. . . .

Alloted space

The underground line I travel into London on is the same one which runs from Heathrow Airport. In fact, my local tube station, Hounslow West, is only a couple of stops down the line. So when my train passes the fields of allotment sites run by Hounslow Council, with their rickety sheds and overgrown plots and bent and weather-beaten owners, it always strikes me that this is the first view foreigners get of British living. And with an untrained eye the allotments could well appear as neat little shanty towns for the urban poor. . . .

It's not unheard of for homeless people to be found living in potting sheds, but ideally council allotment space is available for local residents who wish to grow food. So, if you don't have access to a garden, don't despair. If you live in a small space such as a bedsit or high rise flat or jut feel a bit claustrophobic at home, leaving it all to spend some time tilling the soil is a great escape.

And out in the open air you'll meet your neighbours too. Allotments attract people of all ages and backgrounds. They're great places to while away the hours getting close to the earth and community in which you live. If you're one of those people who always seems to be moving home, even if it's only within the same district, then having your own alloted space will give you a chance to put down some roots.

You'll make new friends. Take time to listen and ask questions and you'll learn about the people and place where you live – what it used to be like – and how 'the times they are a changin'. It'll widen your outlook towards your home town and its people. In our society it's easy to become locked into the habit of only ever meeting and talking to people of our own age group and background. Because allotments attract both the elderly and couples with young children – and the odd person somewhere in between – you'll find yourself opening up to these different people and learning to see life through their eyes as well as your own.

Once your crops start to show themselves, you'll be able to share your Christian faith by sharing your produce with the people you meet. Who knows, a sharing system could develop. Or why not invite a number of your fellow allotment workers for a meal and ask them to bring a dish made out of their own produce? For a break from all this food growing, grow some flowers purely so that their beauty brings a cheery dash of colour to your plot. It'll be a real expression of the joy of life.

Action station

- Read:
  Food for free by Richard Mabey (Collins 1989)
  The Green gardening and cooking guide by Bob Sherman & Carol Bowen (Pan 1990)
  The allotment book by Rob Bullock & Gillie Gould (Macdonald Optima 1988)
  The allotment: its landscape and culture by David Crouch & Colin Ward (Faber, 1988)

- Make a meal using only *objets trouvés* – nettle soup followed by steamed veg or a massive salad with a bowl of fruit to follow – all washed down with a nice cold fruit juice or a home-made herb tea.

- Have a picnic with Christian friends and use

the opportunity to talk and pray about the abundance of food that God has provided for the taking.

- Collect the pips and seeds from whatever you happen to be eating and plant them in wild open spaces.

8
Too Many Cooks

You'd think that with all the money, technology and scientific knowledge that is centred in the developed world, we could rely on a diet that kept us in good health. But unfortunately the reverse is in fact true. 'Evidence is now mounting that a refined, low-fibre, high-fat diet is linked to an increased risk for certain diseases, including heart disease, stroke, obesity and particular forms of cancer.'[1]

Certainly we have tremendous access to different types of food, but with that come plenty of disadvantages too. Many of the foods we eat contain very little nutritional value. For, since the middle of the last century when all the natural goodness was refined out of bread during the milling process, our food has undergone increasing alteration. Indeed, having removed vital ingredients of vitamins, minerals and fibre content, an awful lot of it now has to be put back later in the production process. Perhaps the most cynical of these processes is the brown/white/brown state of sugar and breads. The unrefined, more wholesome raw material is refined to bright whiteness and then coloured brown so that it looks whole-some. Such tampering also pushes up the price of the food both economically *and* healthwise.

More than 5.3 billion packets of crisps are sold every year,[2] which in itself says something about the quality of the British diet. And in the long journey from their humble origin as potatoes, they metamorphize into tasty but terribly unnutritional snacks, of strange flavours like cheese and onion, and Worcester sauce, which in reality have little association with the actual flavour they represent. If you're a vegetarian, I wouldn't worry about the meat content of beef or smoky bacon tasting crisps. Chances are, they've never seen a herd of cattle, let alone even hovered over cooking meat to catch their 'meaty' flavour.

The cheapest food available to us is that which is naturally available. Whether free to be picked, farmed, or combined with other similarly natural ingredients to produce a new dish. God has given us all we need, and there's really no need for us to adulterate it in the hope that we'll somehow improve its flavour or colouring, or extend its shelf life. Just consider the so-called primitive cultures where the land and sea provide for everybody's needs.

But obviously it is not as simple as that. We live in the modern Western world. 'I would prefer to live in a world where we harvested our foods fresh from the earth, ate them immediately and never had to give a thought to food preservatives, arti-ficial emulsifiers and stabilizers, anti-oxidents and permitted colours. Alas, we do not live in such a world. High technology food production and elaborate chains of food distribution have created a situation in which food additives are necessary. Yet for the protection of oneself and one's family it is also necessary to be well informed about these hundreds of additives in quite specific terms and highly aware of the possible implications of their inclusion in our daily diet.'[3]

Certainly there is an increase in the West in eating high-fibre, low-fat foods, but it is slight and largely confined to middle-class consumers who know their onions. Once, doing my shopping in a Kew greengrocer's, I couldn't help smiling when the grocer's young son came scurrying out from the back of the shop pleading, 'Mum, can I have an apple?' Most children pine for sweets! He seemed well on the way to growing up healthy. Seeing the fruit and veg on show anew, I sensed the bright array of oranges, reds and greens that had attracted a child's eye.

Yet in general the food we eat is processed beyond recognition. Or filled with additives that can act like drugs in the human body. 'Some products, especially some foods, are so adulterated by the time they reach the market that they actually constitute a hazard to health.'[4] If you've ever suffered a hyper-active child, if you're anything like me, your gut reaction may well have been along the lines of thinking 'Crumbs, the kid's overdosed on tartrazine', which is the additive that gives drinks like orange squash their garish glow, and sends children in particular haywire.

A rough guide to what food on the supermarket

shelves contains is indicated by ingredients being listed in general in descending order of quantity. Often sugars and starches feature far higher on such lists than the actual product such as fruit. The E-code introduced in 1984 helped make it easier to identify many of the additives in our food. Maurice Hanssen's book *E for additives*[5] is an extremely useful guide to what each E number means.

Land army

But a lot of this adulteration – some of the less harmful arguably necessary to make sure food doesn't go off on supermarket shelves – begins before a product even sees a factory. The mass of chemicals added to soil to help crops grow in the first place are a terrible blight on the environment, though they're poured on in the hope that enough food can be grown: 'Millions of gallons of pesticides and an ever-increasing amount of nitrogen, potash and phosphate fertilizers are poured onto the soil every year. These chemicals, combined with the development of high-technology farming machinery allows us to produce larger yields with a fraction of the previous workforce – and thus more cheaply.'[6]

Yet not only are jobs lost, but the surrounding wildlife and environment can be badly tainted by such farming methods. Crops grow increasingly immune to fertilizers, and so more and more must be added to get the same yield that a smaller dose of the same fertilizer once managed to promote. Fertilizers, including harmful nitrates, leach into the soil and sink into the ground water which collects beneath. This in turn flows into the rivers and streams and ultimately the sea, taking its poisonous load with it. Since the world's amount of water – combined with that in the atmosphere – always remains the same (the water that John used to baptize Jesus is raining on someone today), it must be becoming increasingly polluted.

Nevertheless, make sure any fruit and vegetables are given a good wash and scrub before you eat them, or, better still, consider growing your own so you'll know what goes on them, or buy the unfortunately higher priced organically grown groceries instead if your purse is up to it. If you can't afford it, at least reduce the amount of over-processed foods you do eat, and go for thick-skin-ned fruit and vegetables which hopefully should be less susceptible to contamination from sprays than are many soft fruits.

'Protection of food crops is big business – each year about four billion dollars is spent worldwide on agrochemicals. Over half the money allocated to plant protection goes into insecticides', admitted the industry in a *Time* magazine advertising feature.[7] It's true that on average a sixth of a field of crops is destroyed by insects and pests, so a certain amount of control is necessary, but at the same time it is vital that a lot of thought go into the human and environmental costs of such crop protection. No longer do agrochemicals simply seek out and destroy pests. These days research into plants and insects has led to the concept – and practice – of genetic manipulation, whereby certain

chemicals can alter the mating behaviour of insects
so that they die out in an area, or by inducing
plants to produce proteins that are toxic to the
insects that feed on them. Though these may be
harmless to the surrounding environment, we
must nevertheless be careful that we don't upset
the fine balance of the ecosystem. By killing off a
pest which feeds on crops we could be killing off
the 'higher' life forms which feed on the pest. One
could argue that simply by cultivating a crop over
an area one has disrupted the natural course of
things. It's certainly a brave new world and one
that we must be very careful about tampering
with.

Irradiation sickness

In recent years in a bid to give food a longer shelf-
life and kill bacteria that prey on crops, the issue
of irradiated food has reared its head. Though on
the surface apparently 'a good thing', you don't
have to dig too deep to discover that there are a
great many negative issues involved: 'The main
reason for irradiating food is to cover up deficienc-
ies in quality, hygiene and freshness.'[8]

Indeed, the long-term effects from eating
irradiated food based on experiments involving
animals show disturbing physical side-effects,
including reduced growth, miscarriages, genetic
mutations, heart conditions and haemorrhaging.
A lot of the research that has gone into proving
the usefulness of irradiation has in fact been con-
ducted unreliably.

And though irradiation *can* kill harmful bacteria, there is evidence that it can prove dangerous simply because it has little impact on more strong bacteria. Indeed, the helpful signs God has provided to warn us off bad food, including the growth of mould and an 'off' smell, are irradiated out of existence. And though a few germs and a little bacteria on the whole can do little harm to healthy individuals (in fact the body can grow strong in fighting back), there are sections of our community who would be at definite risk. Young babies, elderly people, pregnant women and those with suppressed immune systems, including people who are HIV positive or have AIDS, and transplant patients, could all be poisoned by the irradiation of bad food.

Yet irradiation could be carried out without us knowing; it is not possible to tell whether food has undergone irradiation or not. In the process of irradiation, food is exposed to doses of ionizing radiation, a by-product of the nuclear industry. The radiation acts as a pesticide and preservative, and also destroys some of the food's nutritional value in the process. Not only this, but produce already contaminated can be given a quick burst of power to make it look like new. Like those creepy fairy stories where the evil queen or step-mother turns a withered, poisoned apple into a juicy piece of fruit to tempt the innocent heroine, irradiated food has a dark past. Many argue that good food, handled and kept in hygienic ways, doesn't need to be irradiated – so the question has to be posed, what are the irradiators trying to hide?

As Sir Julian Rose stated in a letter to *The Times*: 'It should be readily apparent that this is a "high-tech" attempt to paper over the rapidly widening cracks of our modern food production techniques. Food irradiation marks the zenith of misguided technical "fixes" for problems that have to be tackled at source, via a bold and possibly radical reappraisal of the way we produce, handle and distribute our food.'[9]

Unfortunately, whether or not our government is willing to give the go-ahead for irradiation to be carried out in *this* country, there is huge potential for a trade in exporting bad food to the Continent where it can be treated, before bringing it back into the UK where it will be sold as fresh food. Given this disturbing news, it is obviously vitally important that strict import and export controls are enforced to prevent such produce from slipping through the net and into our shopping baskets.

Beef encounters

Meat has come under the microscope recently due to the growing incidence since 1985 of Bovine Spongiform Encephalopathy (BSE), otherwise known as 'mad cow disease', a virus that damages the brains of any infected cattle. MP John Gummer tried to allay the public's fears by force-feeding his daughter a beefburger on the TV news to show how safe eating meat was. But it was a publicity stunt, which like the one involving Mrs Thatcher having bins deliberately emptied so that she could be seen to be picking up litter, understandably backfired. Of course many people took his message with the proverbial pinch of salt; after all, trust in so-called 'experts' had been rather dented when it came out that the spread of BSE in the first place was due to feeding recycled *animal* protein, and in particular sheep brains, to herbivorous cattle!

Feed a herbivore meat and at the very least it is surely going to suffer an upset stomach or two. . . . God didn't create cattle to be omnivores – and through BSE and other viruses and bacteria that poison our food, we are reaping the sorry consequences of going against nature.

The BSE scare, combined with the general ill-feeling about the fat content of red meat, already seems to have taken its toll. In 1989, for the first time chicken outstripped beef as Britain's most popular meat. And then along came salmonella.

First detected in chickens in summer 1988, it soon became apparent that it was also associated with the eggs that they laid. Though salmonella did little harm to the host bird, the number of poisonings it caused among *humans* doubled in one year alone. By the end of 1988 at least five hundred cases of infection were being recorded each week, and twenty-three people died from salmonella poisoning. The Junior Health Minister at the time, Edwina Currie, bit the bullet and warned people not to eat raw eggs or use them in mayonnaise and dressings. But she infuriated the egg industry by declaring that *most* egg production in this country is infected with salmonella, and stepped down as writs flew all around. The salmonella issue quietened down, but that doesn't mean that we should be less careful about cooking our eggs. I generally boil my eggs for about ten minutes. . . .

But contaminants in our farm produce are nothing new. For years growth promoters, hormones and routine antibiotics have been given to animals as part of the intensive farming process. At the same time, at least some of those chemicals have very likely passed along the food chain via the meat on our plates and into our own systems. Not only that, but animal fat is basically unhealthy if we eat too much; it's high in cholesteral. It also accumulates any pesticides, which it has a tendency to absorb and which can harm us further. Evidence of the infamous DDT, for example, has been found as far afield as in the eggs of penguins living in the Antarctic, the shell being too weak to enable the chick to form properly before it breaks. It can be no accident that cancers are so common today. For cancer is the legacy of a life lived in an environment that is chemically unsuitable for life.

Unfortunately the closure of the Bristol-based laboratory of the Institute of Food Research in 1990 has drastically restricted research into the handling and processing of meat from abattoir to microwave. It was the experiments there that identified the potential dangers for the elderly and pregnant women, among others, in microwave cooking, and also their inability to fight back against such bacteria as salmonella and listeria. The Centre was heavily involved with researching into the incidence of salmonella in poultry, and was reported to be close to discovering a way of eradicating it from British poultry altogether when the research work was forced to stop due to lack of financial backing. Obviously a great loss to the nation, and in particular its good health, its absence emphasizes the need for each of us to be very careful about what meat we eat. It is important that meat and eggs are cooked thoroughly before eating, and we need to take care over eating soft cheeses, patés, and pre-cooked meals that are susceptible to contamination; that at the very least they are bought *and* eaten well within their sell-by date.

Whose life is it anyway?

Perhaps the most sinister of cases where too many cooks are working to spoil the broth of foodstuffs naturally available to us, is the patenting of life forms.

Already a 'cancer mouse' – a mouse which has had its genes altered so that it is predisposed to develop cancer – is being marketed in the UK. Biotechnological and legal development now make it possible to cross the characteristics of one animal or plant with another, even though the species are different.

The Brave New World scenario this conjures up is darkened by the very fact that whatever benefits to mankind come to light (and there could be benefits; human insulin for diabetics now costs a fraction of what it once did since an appropriate 'manufactured' insulin was patented), are the product of a patented, that is copyrighted, life form. The company that owns that patent will have power over those who wish to use, say, a

new crop that is resistant to pests. Third World
farmers could be held to ransom, so to speak, by
being forced into further debt from pressures on
them to use the 'new' strains. Very soon they
could find themselves dangerously dependent on
the biotechnological companies for their food
needs.

'How will the European Commission explain to
millions of peasant farmers in the Third World that
the genetic variations developed by their forebears
over countless generations will in future belong to
European companies? Genetic resources must be
considered as our common shared heritage', stated
the World Development Movement's Ed Mayo.[10]

All this tampering with the basic structures of
life obviously has tremendous ethical implications
too. Scientists may truly believe that their research
is furthering the sum of human knowledge, but
funded by multinational corporations that have
little more than a *commercial* interest in the development of new life forms, scientists *must* consider
the consequences of their actions.

For the very idea of research at such a level
reveals a disturbing arrogance concerning man's
superiority over creation. It is the logical con-
clusion to the belief that God is dead. For without
God, anything seems possible; where are the controls that otherwise prevent us from forming an
ultimately fascist view of the world and its inhabitants? Realize that this world actually belongs to
God, and we realize too that patenting life forms
can only have a dangerously high cost for all of
us.

For God's range of plants and creatures *is* limited on this earth. To be dissatisfied with what He has provided for our needs, to wish to dig for more, is to dig ourselves a pit of darkness.

Action station

- Read:

  The Politics of Food by Geoffrey Cannon (Century 1987)

  E for Additives by Maurice Hanssen (Thorsons 1989)

  Food Additives: taking the lid off what we really eat by Erik Millstone (Penguin 1986)

  Food Irradiation: the facts by Tony Webb and Dr Tim Long (Thorsons 1987)

- To keep abreast of scientific developments in the food industry read *New Scientist* magazine.

- For further information on the issue of patenting life-forms write to: The Genetics Forum, 258 Pentonville Road, London N1 9JY.

- For further details about food irradiation and other food issues, contact The London Food Commission, PO Box 291, London N5.

9
Eat Your Greens

Times have changed. Where not so many years ago if you declared yourself a vegetarian you were thought to be a bit strange, a bit of a crank (a term turned to good use as the name of one of the first and perhaps best known of vegetarian eateries), it's eating meat that gets the bad press these days. People worried about heart disease, BSE, salmonella and listeria, not to mention factory farming, are cutting down or saying 'no' more often to their carnivorous tendencies.

The number of vegetarians in the UK has shot up dramatically in the past few years. Once very much a minority interest, as many as three million adults (not to mention their children and the mass of teenage idealists) are now vegetarian, and substantially more people have cut down on their red meat intake.

The meat trade is understandably worried. Not only at one point was there talk of changing butchers' white uniforms to red in order to hide the mark of the beast, but the meat industry has taken to advertising its product in glossy magazines. You can always tell that there's something up when not just a brand, but a whole product has the marketing men behind it. When the Government starts telling us how wonderful our nationalized industries are, we know they're about to be sold off. And it's now the sugar industry's turn to tell us that the white stuff is a vital and natural ingredient of any balanced diet. . . .

But what's vegetarianism got to do with being a Christian? Isn't meat God-given? Didn't Jesus eat fish? Not only have I had 'Vegetarianism isn't biblical' thrown at me in my time (by a holier-than-thou flatmate who just happened to be sleeping with her boyfriend, but I felt it would have been a bit below the belt to throw that one back at her), but a guy I got talking to at a recent party actually declared that there's an evil spirit of vegetarianism. I felt like telling him that I'd heard that there was a spirit against anything that challenged the status quo, but my problem is that I was brought up to be polite, so I bit my tongue instead. (On asking jokingly if he'd read my book *Going Green*, he remarked that he only read books that the Holy Spirit told him to. I doubt he's reading this one either.) I can't really relate to his way of thinking. As Jesus said, it's what's already inside you that's the problem, not what we eat: ' "Don't you see that whatever enters the mouth goes into the stomach and then out of the body? But the things that come out of the mouth come from the heart, and these make a man 'unclean'." '[1]

In fact, in the prelapsarian Garden of Eden, that is the time before Adam and Eve chose to flout God's Law, vegetarianism was certainly very much part of the lifestyle. Humans and animals lived in harmony with God. God had provided for all our needs and meat was simply not on the menu. 'Then God said, "I give you every seed-bearing plant on the face of the whole earth and every tree that has fruit with seed in it. They will be yours for food. And to all the beasts of the earth and all the creatures that move on the ground – everything that has the breath of life in it – I give every green plant for food." And it was so.'[2]

But our split with God was simultaneous with our split with nature. Humanity disobeyed God and went against nature by eating of the tree that was not meant to be eaten from. The world was turned on its head. And following the Flood, and having literally washed the slate clean, God told Noah of the new arrangement on the planet: ' "The fear and dread of you will fall upon all the beasts of the earth and all the birds of the air, upon every creature that moves along the ground, and upon all the fish of the sea; they are given into your hands. Everything that lives and moves will be food for you. Just as I gave you the green plants, I now give you everything." '[3]

Fancy a polar bear burger, or a slice of golden retriever with roast potatoes and sprouts, anyone? I can just picture the pair of cattle arguing between themselves as they grazed together once they'd left the Ark: 'You're not telling me that we came all this way just to end up on somebody's plate?'!

Meat is murder?

So if God's given us the go-ahead to indulge in the odd bit of flesh, why should anyone choose not to eat it? Clearly the 'Meat is murder', 'Thou shalt not kill anything' line that gets bandied about at animal rights meetings cannot be that of the Christian. For if killing an animal for food is murder, then choosing to kill an animal for any other purpose must be too. It places animals on a par with humans, and since God has given us the role of steward of His Creation, including His animals, then in a Christian sense that can surely not be so. It can also lead to a dangerous way of thinking that justifies people being killed or dying to save animal lives.

Most people concerned with animal welfare do not go along with the extremist fringe who threaten the lives of, say, vivisectionists. For if you believe that man is an animal, then to hurt a person makes you as bad as they in their poor treatment of non-human creatures. Yet I have been to talks on vegetarianism and to 'living without cruelty'-type discussions, and overheard people quite openly say that it would be better if sick people needing extensive treatment die rather than expose animals to the cruelty of vivisection. And I've never quite understood how people in the Green movement can be pro-animal rights and also pro-abortion. It makes animal life more sacred than that of humans.

A growing number of Christians are choosing not to eat meat. They accept that there's nothing fundamentally wrong with being an omnivore. Yet as Christians we *should* be concerned about animal welfare. After all, God is. 'Are not two sparrows sold for a penny? Yet not one of them will fall to the ground apart from the will of your Father.'[4] Christian vegetarians recognize also that in this modern age our methods of animal husbandry leave a lot to be desired, that meat eating keeps the Third World harnessed by the chains of poverty, and meat eating these days is quite a health hazard in itself.

But being a Christian *and* a vegetarian has only recently begun to be accepted as a valid option. For some, the fact that somebody is a veggie is curious enough. Indeed, there are times when I've been somebody's guest who, not knowing my eating habits, has presented me with a plate of meat. In such circumstances I eat it. Not every veggie would go along with me, but the way I see it is that if someone has taken the time, trouble and expense to rustle something up for me, then it's not fair on them for me to cause a scene. Mind you, the worst scenario I've come across is when having decided that I'm going to eat the meat that's been put in front of me, I've my fork poised at my mouth about to take a bite when some helpful person blurts out, 'Oh, didn't you know, Catherine's a vegetarian'! The poor host is thoroughly embarrassed, and flustered pulls away my plate, and I'm left with my hand in mid-air, unsure whether to eat the hovering morsel of meat or not. I can assure you that if I've got to this point, it's because me and my conscience have reached a satisfactory agreement. Those 'helpful' spoken words would be better left unsaid.

Admittedly there have been times when someone has presented me with a plate of fish and defiantly declared to me that vegetarians most certainly *do* eat fish. I'm afraid that on such occasions my sheer bloodymindedness surfaces and I refuse to touch the stuff. I'm not altogether sure that this is the most appropriate action for a Christian.

There must be some disreputable eating places where untouched food is reheated and re-presented at another table. But in general, particularly if you're eating at someone's house, the untouched food on your plate will be considered spoiled, and be scraped into the kitchen pedal bin. Which does nothing for the animal concerned. In my mind, you might as well have eaten it. Admittedly, some vegetarians or vegans can't stomach meat. I love the stuff.

I was once standing on a platform at Euston Station feeling rather hungry when I happened to spot a large billboard advert for British Rail breakfasts. My eyes scanned a massive picture of a regular fry-up: fat juicy sausages, a long rasher of bacon and some mushrooms, and I gazed at the image, licked my lips and thought 'I could *kill* one of those'.

But it's because of my concern for animals that I choose not to. This was brought home to me anew one recent autumn evening. We'd had mice in our kitchen, and with three men in the household there was a lot of macho talk about poison and setting traps. Somehow in all the talk the mouse managed to evolve into a huge rat, so my plea for the use of a humane trap which would enable us to deposit the live creature at the end of a very long garden, to live out its days in peace, fell on very deaf ears. The night before Guy Fawkes, when everybody was out, I'd been to a concert at my church and walked home to our old Victorian vicarage alone in the dark. I made myself a cup of tea, and pondering in the kitchen just happened to glance at the small mousetrap that had been set. We'd had already had a couple of false alarms on previous evenings when the trap had sprung of its own accord. This evening, on my own in that macabre setting, I found what everybody else had been hoping for: a dead mouse which had been caught by the wire of the trap between the eyes as it had sniffed at the cheese.

And as I took the trap out into the dark of our garden to release the body, it struck me that that was why I was a vegetarian; because there was no need for that mouse to be killed, and there's no need for animals to be killed for my food.

But whether as a Christian you have chosen to eat meat or not, be careful not to look down on those who choose to eat differently from you. 'The man who eats everything must not look down on him who does not, and the man who does not eat everything must not condemn the man who does, for God has accepted him.'[5]

I once tried veganism (when I was living with the flatmate who thought vegetarianism was theologically dodgy, so I probably was asking for it!). Not only did I find it quite dull (I do like the strong flavours of eggs and cheese), but every time somebody opened the fridge and spotted my slab of tofu, they would wonder aloud at its biblical significance, and I would have to justify my diet. And then it was decided that because I only ate vegetables, my faith was obviously weak.[6]

Thanks Paul! Actually, further in his letter to the Romans he concludes that an action truly done for God is what matters; which is why we should be prepared to accept our differences of opinion, action and conscience. 'He who eats meat, eats to the Lord, for he gives thanks to God, and he who abstains does so to the Lord and gives thanks to God.'[7] Both are good in God's sight.

Hungry for heifers?

The more one investigates what really goes on behind the scenes of the meat industry, the desire to stop eating meat grows stronger. Even if the inherent cruelty to animals doesn't stir one's conscience, we should consider the background of importing grain from other countries to feed the cattle which eventually make it to our plates.

Not only is five times as much valued land needed to feed a meat-eater than a vegetarian, but the millions of tons of grain which must feed our farm animals every year are imported from developing countries such as Brazil and West Africa, which would be better off using that land on which to feed their people: 'About thirty-six million acres of the Third World is developed for the production of animal feed for European live-stock.'[8]

Clearly we *must* bear this in mind. Meat-eating is a tremendously inefficient form of protein for humans in a world where a growing human population must live off a limited amount of land. Certainly we could argue for us humans to restrict our growth a bit. There are now more than five *billion* of us on this planet. And as the greatest consumers of world resources, we in the West should seriously consider limiting the number of children we have, and if we wish to have a large family, be prepared to adopt instead. Christians without children, whether single or married, who aren't in a position to adopt or foster a child could choose to sponsor one instead through an organization like Action Aid or Tear Fund. Although a child will be singled out for you to sponsor, the money you donate will go towards helping the whole community. Some people buy pets to keep them company. Cats in particular are popular among professional young women. But pets eat an awful lot of meat too. Some of the most preferred brands of cat food are practically all meat or fish; some people's pet cats eat better than people in this country and in the developed world. Redress the balance by adopting a Third World granny through Help the Aged, or supporting a child in the developing world, and concentrate your energies on building a relationship through letters with a person overseas. Learn about their country and culture so that you can pray for them and their family with understanding and a growing love.

Keep fit

Some people claim that being a vegetarian can prove unhealthy; that you can never be sure that you're getting all the vitamins and minerals necessary for sound physical and mental fitness. Certainly vegetarians do need to be careful, but their needs *can* be met by their non-meat diet. Indeed, vegetarians, simply because they must check lists of ingredients to make sure food isn't contaminated by dead animals, are perhaps more conscious than most of their dietary needs. 'Eating vegetables is for adventure-some people; people who look at a new food the same way they look at a book that hasn't been read or a hill that needs climbing.'[9]

Vegetarians who eat dairy produce and eggs are less at risk from poor diet than vegans who subsist on a diet that contains no animal products whatsoever, but then vegans would argue in their own favour. Basically, whether we're meat eaters, vegetarians or vegans we should be aware of what we're putting into our stomachs and whether or not it's going to do us good. There are certainly lots of good cookery books and helpful organizations that provide useful information about health and fitness for those on non-meat diets, so there's really no excuse not to be informed about good food. Whether or not you choose to stick to healthy eats is another matter. After all, you could be a vegetarian or vegan on a diet of veggie burgers and chips!

One could argue that it's safer to be a vegetarian

than a meat eater. For a start, more than nine in ten of recorded food poisoning cases can be traced to eating meat. Indeed many of God's laws regarding eating set out in the Old Testament to instruct the Jews (I suppose the Bible must be one of the first 'lifestyle' books) were as much about how to stay healthy in a tough rural environment as about being strict religious laws. Under such conditions, it's not a good idea to cook all your dishes using the same pots; contamination can spread from one food to another. Similarly, having given us permission to eat animals, God is very clear about what part of the meat isn't healthy: 'You must not eat meat that has its lifeblood still in it'.[10] Blood can spread infection very easily. To drink animals' blood, though in an emergency it might prove nutritious, is also potentially very dangerous.

There are non-meat foodstuffs such as kidney beans which need to be cooked properly before being eaten if one is to avoid being ill, but in general veggies have little to fear if they wash their fruit and veg thoroughly before they prepare a meal. In the Bible Daniel and his companions refrained from eating meat for ten days, living on a herbal diet and water to drink[11], and it didn't do them any harm!

Yet when you hear of the bugs that meat eaters must look out for these days – salmonella, BSE, listeria, not to mention all the hormones and antibiotics that are routinely added to the factory farmed animals as they await their fate – one wonders why omnivores act so concerned about the health of vegetarians. Non-meat eaters tend to carry less body fat than meat eaters, and are also less likely to suffer from breast cancer, heart attacks or high blood pressure.

Once one gets interested in these specialist diets you hear about intriguing ways of improving your health by limiting your diet to certain foodstuffs. A lot of vegetarians choose to go a step further and become vegans. Some people go as far as choosing to eat only fruit. A macro-biotic diet certainly *sounds* healthy in an earthy beans-and-lentils sort of way. It is not specifically vegetarian; fish is included in the diet, but there is a strong emphasis on eating fried vegetables and plenty of grains and cereals, and theoretical emphasis on the idea of balancing the food one eats. For at the very basis of the macro-biotic diet is the belief in the balance of Yin and Yang, which is claimed to occur naturally in a whole grain of rice. If that's the case, then I'd take it with a pinch of salt.

The idea behind Yin and Yang is that everything has its complementary opposite; negative/positive, moon/sun, female/male, and I presume by the same way of thinking, good/evil, heaven/hell and God/the Devil too. The theory goes that there are two sides to every coin, so to speak. Which has nothing to do with the Christian faith. Surely our hope is that good can exist without evil, health without suffering, love without hate, God without the Devil. . . . No one needs to follow a macro-biotic diet and the thinking behind it in order to be healthy. A good balanced diet of fresh food, including plenty of fruit and vegetables which have been processed as little as possible, and a reduced fat, high fibre content, is a diet designed by God to keep us well in body, mind and, with our eyes on Him, in spirit too.

Action station

- Read:
  The Vegetarian Handbook edited by Jane Bowler (Vegetarian Society 1990)
  Why Vegan? the ethics of eating and the need for change by Kath Clements (GMP 1985)
  The Vegetable Year Cookbook by Judy Ridgeway (Piatkus 1985)

- For further details regarding vegetarianism and veganism, write to The Vegetarian Society UK Ltd, Parkdale, Dunham Road, Altrincham, Cheshire WA14 4QG or The Vegan Society, 7 Battle Road, St Leonards-on-Sea, East Sussex TN37 7AA.

- Contact Animal Aid, 7 Castle Street, Tonbridge, Kent TW9 1BH for details of their 'Make Your Next Meal Count' campaign.

- If you're happy eating meat, why not reduce your meat intake? Try eating vegetarian food more often. Eat cuts of animals rather than whole ones.

10
Factory Flaw

Though it's OK for us as Christians to eat meat, many people, whether believers or not, are limiting the amount of meat they consume. Not just because they're worried about the dangers of contamination from bacteria, but also because of a genuine concern for the way animals are treated on their way to the dinner plate.

'Whether or not we believe that human beings have a moral right to eat animals, we should be aware that animals are now bred, reared and killed in a way which is entirely different from that conjured up by the happy farmyard scenes of our children's books. Battery hens are crammed into overcrowded cages without enough room to flap their wings; dairy cows are robbed of their offspring within a few days of giving birth; many veal calves are kept in tiny crates in virtual darkness.'[1]

Certainly God has made us in His image and given us dominion over the animal kingdom,[2] but as His ambassadors on this earth He has also given us responsibility to take care of it for Him. Certainly He doesn't mind us eating animals, but He minds how we treat the creatures we farm for that purpose. ' "What do you think? If a man owns a hundred sheep, and one of them wanders away, will he not leave the ninety-nine on the hills and go and look for the one that wandered off? And if he finds it, I tell you the truth, he is happier about that one sheep than about the ninety-nine that did not wander off." '[3] Jesus' parable about God's concern for the individual soul is as much an expression of the concern that a shepherd should have for each sheep in the flock under his care.

The impression we generally have of how we would like to see farm animals kept, absorbed from biblical imagery and children's picture books, is far removed from the often clinical yet barbaric practices of the modern world. The original intention of keeping animals closely together was an attempt to make the best possible use of the space available while at the same time increasing the production of meat. Yet the downside was that the increased stress on the animals reduced the quality of the meat, stock were injured in the caging process, and disease spread like wildfire through the pens. And though antibiotics *were* added to feed in an attempt to reduce the risk of infection, resistant strains such as salmonella withstood the onslaught and fought back in a devastating manner.

'Each year some 450 *million* animals are killed for food in Britain. Most spend all or the greater part of their lives in entirely artificial conditions, unable to satisfy their natural desire for movement and contact with their own kind. Some are imprisoned for their products rather than their flesh: hens are crammed, as many as five at a time into battery cages without room enough for even one to spread her wings; cows are subjected to yearly pregnancies and then robbed of their calves so that humans can drink their milk. Eventually when egg or milk yields cease to be 'economical', the animals are killed, their less than prime flesh being used for pet and junk food.'[4]

It is also much cheaper to keep animals in such poor conditions: 'During the last thirty years or more, farmers have been under increasing pressure to tailor traditional farming methods to the needs of "cost-effective" production. This has meant in practice a dramatic increase in the number of animals used, a tendency to specialize in one form of production, and, more usually than not, systems of close confinement. Farming animals intensively has become the norm.'[5]

So prices of meat, eggs, milk and dairy products produced in factory farm conditions are kept artificially low because through our purchases of such foodstuffs we allow the inhumane situation to continue. Admittedly if you're on a low income it *is* difficult to make positive choices about what you buy. I don't mind paying extra for my free-range eggs when I can afford them; I'm quite happy then to put principle over pocket (and I do balance it out by not buying meat, so that my food bill as a single person comes to between £10 and £15 per week, which is pretty good going), but on the dole my Green principles had to go to the wall. I simply couldn't *afford* to pay nearly a quid for six eggs.

Nevertheless, in supermarkets where free-range eggs have been sold alongside battery-farmed eggs, many customers have chosen to pay more for the cruelty-free eggs, because they know what they're buying into. If we want animals to be treated better – and as Christians we should – then we must be prepared to pay more.

'Those of us who remain carnivores can at least show our concern by talking to our butchers, whether we're lucky enough to have a small, independent one or a high-street chain or a supermarket. We can ask them whether they are happy about the way their animals are reared and slaughtered,' suggested the *Church Times'* correspondent, Sarah Stancliffe, 'We can tell them that we would be prepared to pay more for good quality meat and to balance our budgets by not eating meat every day. They can then encourage the farmers to improve their methods.'[6]

The Farm Animal Welfare Council has drawn up a code of welfare for farm animals in terms of five freedoms:–

1) Freedom from malnutrition
2) Freedom from thermal or physical discomfort
3) Freedom from injury or disease
4) Freedom to express most normal, socially acceptable patterns of behaviour
5) Freedom from fear.[7]

It might sound a bit idealistic, but it is one worth working towards, and takes account of the conditions of animals in captivity, regardless of the reason for their confinement and whether they are kept under free-range or intensive husbandry systems. It is a wise code of conduct for anyone who keeps animals, particularly farmers, and one that the Government would do well to make law.

As stewards of God's creation, Christians should be at the forefront of making a stand against such cruel factory practices, but we are often far behind. 'The Church Commissioners, for example, own and lease over 160,000 acres of farming land. Under present legislation, animals can be subject to intensive farming, and are so on Church-owned land. It is anomalous that the Church of England should allow on its land farming practices which many senior ecclesiastics oppose . . . It is sad to see the Church wrong-footed in a debate to which it has so much to contribute.'[8]

Battery operated

The much reported onslaught of disease and its impact on farm animals has been particularly evident among egg-laying hens. Not only have whole flocks of birds been affected – and infected – but they have passed the infection through to their offspring too. Neither factory farm nor free-range are completely safe, though among free-range farms, salmonella is generally easier to control. Farmer Martin Pitt, whose free-range eggs are sold in many health food stores, not only has hens that are so clever that, in the same way that there's a guy in the M & M sweet factory whose job it is to print the initials on every chocolate, they stamp every egg they lay with the name of the farm in red ink (I suppose it's a bit like tramps leaving signs to let others know where kind people live), but he once covered the box with a large red sticker declaring the legend 'Salmonella free'. It was enough that my flatmate Jim would joke about the photo on all my egg boxes showing, as the caption read, 'Hens *enjoying* the free-range conditions'. 'They're obviously happy chickens!' he'd smirk. I imagine in the battery farms that it's practically impossible to guarantee the health of one's birds.

In fact, when the battery system of farming was first introduced, the intention was to *improve* the health of hens and so produce more eggs. The battery cage separated the birds from their own droppings and so prevented much disease. Birds were kept one to a cage but eventually more were added. Adult hens have a wing span of at least thirty inches, but a popular cage size for live birds is now a miniscule 18" × 20" and in general houses *five* birds. Around forty million hens live like this.

Understandably disease spreads rapidly between hens in such close quarters, and cooped up in such inhumane conditions that the natural order of things is grossly over-emphasized to horrific effect. The 'pecking order' of hierarchy among chickens, which isn't necessarily nice to witness even in the best conditions, as birds bully each other, is brutalized even further by the cramped conditions. The weak have nowhere to escape from their oppressors, the quality of eggs is reduced by the intense stress of the situation, and chemicals – vitamins, hormones and stimulants – must be added to improve the flavour of the eggs. Often birds are debeaked shortly after hatching, to cut down the damage they inflict upon each other, but this is a painful and shocking treatment. Birds are crippled as they perch on the wire cages. It is all a long, long way from the relative comforts experienced by free-range hens.

'A happy free-range chicken able to scratch around for its food and choosing many different pigment-containing and mineral-rich items, will usually produce richly golden and strongly shelled eggs. The less fortunate battery hens have to rely upon what is in their feed to give their eggs colour.'[9]

Yet if you're intent on eating cruelty-free eggs, make sure that the box is labelled 'free-range'. Many eggs are said to be 'farm fresh' in order to conjure up images in our minds of those happy chickens scratching around the yard. But such a term is as meaningless as calling something 'environmentally friendly'. Both terms are meant to pacify the shopper into a sense of complacency.

Yet if one is vegetarian, then one must seriously consider what happens to all the male chickens that have no laying purpose and therefore serve no commercial purpose on either battery or free-range farms. Often they end up on someone's plate. It's enough to turn you vegan! In fact, all animal products – eggs, milk, cheese, butter, honey – are tainted with death somewhere along the line. The vast majority of beef that is eaten, for instance, is a by-product of dairy farms; the surplus calves borne by the cow in order to keep her supply of milk on tap in general end up at the slaughterhouse very early on or join a veal or beef herd to be eaten a short while later.

The veal thing

If most people find it difficult to make a stand against other forms of animal abuse, many have a gut reaction against eating veal precisely because of the way veal calves are farmed. Such people declare that were it on a menu where they happened to be eating, they would avoid it. Others would avoid the restaurant. This is certainly a step in the right direction and one from which people can be prompted to think about how animals are forced to suffer from our day-to-day eating patterns. Indeed, just by drinking cows' milk we are actually promoting the veal market.

A succulent white meat, the quality of veal is directly related to the confinement of young male calves in narrow crates. Surplus to the dairy industry and unsuitable for beef, they are literally unable to see the light of day or feel the grass grow beneath their feet. Fed an all-liquid, low-iron diet their flesh remains a sickly pallor that is considered 'ideal' for veal, and sold in the main to the hotel and restaurant business. Denied the roughage their bodies need, these intelligent creatures often end up nibbling their wooden crates or even eating their own hair for nourishment. At fourteen weeks, ready for slaughter, they are weak, often suffering from abcesses and ulcers, and a travesty of what a healthy calf is.

Dutch veal in particular is notoriously farmed under such conditions, and though the tortious crates were banned in the UK in 1990, four in ten of the calves exported by lorry to the Continent are reimported as veal meat for the home market.

Increasingly there has been a move towards a more humane way of producing veal, and though calves must still be kept under cover, on some farms they are allowed to mingle among themselves instead of being housed in the inhumane crate system. The meat is less white as the calves are fed a diet that includes iron, but customers who feel they must eat this type of meat are beginning to favour the off-white version over the so-called 'pure' farmed brands. Since veal, like tuna – the fishing of which leads to the mass-drowning of dolphins caught in unbreakable nets – is a luxury meat, it surely wouldn't be that much of a sacrifice simply to avoid buying it in the first place. . . .

Lambs to the slaughter

Killing can never be tidy. The survival instinct is too strong to allow complacency in any creature about to be killed. They struggle and make the whole thing potentially very messy.

In slaughterhouses, animals are legally meant to be stunned unconscious before they are bled. For cows that means a bolt fired into the brain. Pigs and sheep have to endure low voltage electric tongs hold on each side of their head for seven seconds, and hens are shackled upside down by their feet to a conveyor belt chain which drags their heads through a water bath charged with low voltge electricity. None of these ways is pleasant, none can be or is a hundred per cent successful. And then the creatures, whether they've been stunned or not, have their throats cut.

However slim the safeguards are at the moment in this country, they threaten to be relaxed even further come the opening of the European market from 1992. Animals exported live from the British Isles onto the Continent have long since experienced the harsh conditions of transportation through European countries. But additionally without tough legislation, some species, in particular horses, ponies, mules and donkeys, which since the fifties have not been exported from the UK because of the harsh methods of treatment, transport and slaughter which would be meted out to them, could be included in the new open market. It is important that we support the animal welfare societies which are working to ensure more humane treatment during life and at the point of death for Europe's farm animals.

We're used to seeing new lambs happily frolicking alongside their mothers on our hillsides. It is a view to delight in. Yet the offspring of most farm animals, and indeed the mothers themselves, must face cruel confinement for most if not all of their short lives.

Life is tough for sows. They are confined individually in narrow stalls or tethered in rows by girth straps attached to the concrete floor. Intelligent and gentle animals, they struggle painfully and hopelessly to free themselves from their shackles. Many express mental distress through a repetitive pattern of gnawing at the bars of their stalls. It is in such close and degrading confinement that even heavily pregnant sows must spend their days.

Although the European Parliament voted against this system being continued in the EC in early 1987, the EC has since produced a set of proposals that ignore the Parliament's original recommendations. Though the UK government has agreed to phase out sow stalls and fetters by the end of this century, pressure still needs to be put on the EC to outlaw this inhumane practice throughout the European Community.

Almost all chickens or turkeys destined for our Sunday dinner or Christmas meal plates are farmed intensively. And they're generally just seven weeks old when they're slaughtered, having been bred and reared in the huge windowless sheds of the broiler house among as many as a staggering 100,000 birds. Of the 500 million chickens raised annually in such conditions, twenty to fifty million die before reaching slaughter age, many of them trampled by other birds, or, among turkeys in particular, the victims of cannibalism or disease. A further 2.5 million birds die on their way to the processing plant as a result of injury, suffocation or shock.

Quite clearly from the evidence, it can be seen that most farm animals suffer a great deal in their journey from birth to our plates. As Christians it is vital that we take care to consider the amount of suffering, and as stewards of God's Creation, make sure we work towards alleviating it.

'It seems to me that the only satisfactory basis

on which we can oppose systems of close confinement is by recourse to the argument drawn from *theos* – rights. To put it at its most basic; animals have a God-given right to be animals. The natural life of a Spirit-filled creature is a gift from God. When we take over the life of an animal to the extent of distorting its natural life for no other purpose than our own gain, we fall into sin. There is no clearer blasphemy before God than the perversion of His creatures. To the question "Why is it wrong to deny chickens the rudimentary requirements of their natural life, such as freedom of movement or association?" there is therefore only one satisfactory answer. Since an animal's natural life is a gift from God, it follows that God's right is violated when the natural life of His creatures is perverted.'[10]

Action station

- Read:
  Christianity and the rights of animals by Andrew Linzey (SPCK 1987)
  The kind food guide by Audrey Eyton (Penguin 1987)

- For further information about factory farming and humane alternatives, contact Compassion in World Farming, or its youth branch Farmwatch, 20 Lavant Street, Petersfield, Hampshire GU32 3EW, or Animal Aid, 7 Castle Stret, Tonbridge, Kent TN9 1BH.

- If you have enough space and time, consider

providing a sanctuary for battery hens and other factory-farmed creatures that are past their sell-by date. Contact an organization such as Chickens Lib, PO Box 2, Holmfirth, Huddersfield HD7 1QT for further information.

- If all this information has set your blood boiling about the way we abuse animals for often unnecessary purposes, contact The Vegan Society, 7 Battle Road, St Leonards-on-Sea, East Sussex TN37 7AA for a free Vegan Information Pack. Enclose an A4 size SAE.

- To be in touch with others who have a Christian perspective on animal welfare, contact Animal Christian Concern: May Tripp, 46 St Margarets Road, Horsforth, Leeds LS18 5PG, or Quaker Concern for Animal Welfare: Martin Howard, Webbs Cottage, Woolpits Road, Saling, Braintree, Essex CM7 5DZ for further information. Remember to include an SAE.

11
The Starving Hungry

From an early age many young Western children are encouraged to eat up their meals by recognizing how fortunate they are compared with the world's starving millions. It's not as if any food that's left on the plate can be packed up and shipped overseas, but the child is given an elementary lesson in relating to people on the other side of the world, which the enlightened parent or teacher would do well to build on.

I once watched one part in a series of documentaries that focused on the seven ages of mankind. A bright child amongst a group of largely working class ten year olds from Leeds seemed particularly socially aware. It turned out that when one day he'd moaned to his mother about what he didn't have, she took him along to the local Oxfam shop and showed him the pictures in the window, of children who *really* didn't have anything. . . .

It's certainly a step in the right direction, but it is not enough for us as Christians to *be* concerned. God wants to see results: 'Suppose a brother or sister is without clothers and daily food. If one of you says to him, ''Go, I wish you well; keep warm and well fed'', but does nothing about his physical needs, what good is it? In the same way, faith by itself, if it is not accompanied by action, is dead.'[1]

Though civil wars, unjust governments, and poor climate in the Third World *do* have a strong impact on the health of people living in particular countries, one of the major reasons for the continued hunger of people living in the Third World is the trading structures and financial systems that are centred in the wealthy First World. And as residents of that rich, Western world we have bought into that imbalanced set-up: 'The food we buy supports methods of food production that affect not just our own health, but also the health of the soil and the well-being of people in poorer countries. We need to find a way of eating which minimizes human and animal suffering while keeping ourselves and our planet healthy.'[2]

Indeed we do. For our present system of buying produce – all that exotic fruit, beverages like cocoa, coffee, tea and chocolate – involves large companies buying up vast sections of poor countries, turning them over to what have become known as 'cash crops' and employing local people at a very cheap rate to work there. The best soil feeds the food ready to be shipped to the First World, while the local residents must depend on what they can scrape from the remaining poor earth which soon turns to dust.

Everything is against them. Many Third World countries continue to be faced with crippling debts as they attempt to pay back the money lent to them by the World Bank over a decade ago. There seems little hope; many have repaid the original sum borrowed several times over, but now any money must go towards paying off the interest on the loan, which has grown over the years. The Old Testament Jubilee laws of cancelling debts after a number of years comes into sharp focus here. Put into action today it would release the world's poor countries from the heavy burden of hard debt, and enable them to lift themselves out of poverty by investing the now spare money in the home economy. For until such countries are released from their stifling debts, there will be a limited number of jobs, school places and hospitals for the native population to help lift them out of poverty.

Without money or good land for food, people must salvage, scavenge and search further afield. They chop trees for much-needed firewood, and the land beneath, now without cover, turns to dust and desert. And the malnourished, weak in mind and body, are the nation's suffering heritage.

'At home and overseas, people go hungry, not because there is not enough food available, but because for one reason or another they do not have access to it. Every society has its own rules about who is entitled to what. Usually this depends upon factors like whether a person owns property or land, whether they are unemployed, how much they earn and how many dependants they have.'[3]

Hungry for change

But what can I do? The problems of poverty across the world seem insurmountable. More than twenty million people die every year because they don't have enough to eat, while European nations, including our own, stockpile mountains of grain and lakes of milk because there's too much produced to be used. It is a ludicrous and obscene situation.

And if in the light of that information our own small gestures of trying to change the world seem worthless, think how Bob Geldof must feel! All that energy he put into mobilizing and motivating people into doing something positive for the Third World must at times seem an utter waste. (Mind you, I recall shortly after the 1986 famine discussing the issue of world hunger with my sister Jane. 'How was God helping all those people dying of starvation?' she turned to me in anger. But practically before she'd got the question out of her mouth, there was a light of realization in her face, and, subdued, she answered her own question: 'Bob Geldof.' I'm sure too that there were many miracles and answers to prayer happening all the time among African Christians suffering from hunger, stories we may never get to hear this side of Heaven). In the meantime, the Third World continues to get poorer, people continue to starve, and governments don't seem to change their ways.

'Whether it is the relative poverty in the West, or the greater poverty found in poor nations, we live in a world where hunger is a daily reality for millions of people. Yet it is easy for those of us with so much to be hardened against the agony which hunger brings to others. And the guilt we feel because we are not starving can so quickly paralyze our actions. We want to respond, but we don't know how.'[4]

When one looks at how the world functions there's no doubt that in the West we should, on the whole, be very grateful for our high standard of living. It is a real case of 'there but for the grace of God go I'. But that should motivate us to respond to the 'Two-Thirds' world in our own communities and on the other side of the planet. I personally couldn't and wouldn't go so far as to *thank* God for my lifestyle; I can't help but be aware that our Western way of life is only attainable at the cost of exploiting most of the world's people. We buy their labour, produce, raw materials and land at rock bottom prices to satisfy our own insatiable greed. It is surely our place to ask God's forgiveness for treating His world this way. And we should also be pretty thankful that being involved in such an obviously unjust set-up we happen to find ourselves on the side that benefits from it. You only have to see the cold figures huddled in the shop doorways of our city streets to realize that it's not at all difficult to trip over the edge.

We can respond to the earth's hungry people, not just by making sure we eat everything on our plate and seeing that nothing goes to waste, as we were told to do as kids, but conversely and more importantly, by cutting down on the food that exploits our neighbours. 'To satisfy the insatiable meat demands of the West, forty per cent of the world's cereal harvest goes to feed livestock. It actually takes 10lb of grain to produce one pound of beef. At least thirty times as many people can be supported on a vegetarian diet, yet at any one time over 500 million people throughout the world are seriously malnourished.'[5] It's ironic that the meat industry should use the slogan 'Meat to live' as part of its glossy campaign to woo back the punters. Clearly it is eating meat that is killing people.

Each one of us can work to make something of a difference, however small our gesture seems. By keeping abreast of current affairs across the world our prayers become more focused as our concern grows for particular places.

Solving the problem of world hunger has a lot to do with willing. Not in a New Age Hunger Project type of way, thinking that if enough people simply *believe* that everybody in the world should have enough to eat it will be 'an *idea* whose time has come', but willing that *demands* action,. The Western world certainly has the technology to shift mountains of grain to the Third World, but economic principles that say you can't simply hand out grain to the needy overrule any thought that doing that would save people's lives.

Yet it was charity that kept alive the people of devastated Cambodia, who would otherwise have died of malnutrition and disease because the war-torn nation, ripped apart by Pol Pot's terrifying Khmer Rouge regime, has been denied any relief or developmental aid from governments at an international level. The country, its social structures and communications decimated under the tyranny, had no foundations on which to rebuild itself. They were left to start from scratch.

So we *can* do something by supporting development organizations such as CAFOD, Tear Fund or Christian Aid who work alongside the poor of the world and recognize that the underlying causes of poverty, such as debt and unjust trading patterns, must be addressed as well as financial aid provided. We can campaign by writing to our local and Euro MPs, backed up by information gleaned from such publications as *New Internationalist* magazine, and organizations like the World Development Movement. We can aim to live more simple lifestyles, questioning the materialism of the West which thrives on the backs of the world's poor, both here and overseas. We can buy produce from Traidcraft, Tearcraft and Oxfam which supports the actual communities who make it. And we can be part of the solution instead of part of the problem.

War-torn world

When famine strikes a country we often automatically assume that lack of rainfall is a major reason. While a continent like Africa is subject to extremes of climate, it is in fact a very fertile place; high temperatures and bursts of rainfall are ideal for growth. Admittedly there are regions where the rains don't always come when they're due, which puts tremendous pressure on any community to survive. Yet nations such as Uganda, once hailed by Winston Churchill as the 'pearl of Africa', have been devastated not by drought, but by more obviously man-made disaster. Both Presidents Amin *and* Obote destroyed that nation with their organized terrorism. Ironically, just when Uganda was beginning to get back on its feet under the more civilized President Museveni, along came AIDS which has devastated communities; in many villages only the elderly and their infant grandchildren remain, for the most agriculturally productive members of the local society have died from what has become known as 'Slim'. Aerial photographs grimly reveal that the swift onslaught of AIDS can be easily detected by the way nature is quickly reclaiming previously cultivated areas. . . .

In Africa as in Europe many borders of countries divide tribes or put traditional enemies within the same boundaries, which ultimately leads to the kind of civil unrest of the type witnessed in 1991 in Yugoslavia, when Serbs and Croatians went to war against each other. As the Soviet Union and its communist neighbours began to crumble, and small states asserted their right to independence, the map of Europe began to look very similar to that of before the First World War. For the concept of countries and borders is a very abstract one which can be subverted for good or evil. We are no different from people in Bosnia and Herzegovina, so there should be no need to fight with them or anyone else, which is why having a pen-pal in a different country is such a good idea. In the same way, people can choose to ignore country boundaries but in a negative way recognize tribal or political differences, which at its worst can lead to civil war.

A country already unstable due to lack of rainfall or disease can be plunged into famine when it goes to war. People and resources that would be put to better use in feeding people and keeping them educated and well are invested in the pursuit of killing. Which is exactly what's gone on in the Ethiopia/Eritrean War that has claimed so many lives on and off the battlefield.

In our little corner of the world

If 'charity begins at home' and 'home is where the heart is' as the sayings go, then a good starting point for being aware and responding to hungry people's needs is among our own neighbours. Ask God to open your eyes to those living without, and He'll show you the young single mother, the widowed pensioner, the family whose breadwinner has been made redundant, the student, the homeless person. . . . They're there in our midst trying to make ends meet. For there are malnourished and starving people in our so-called developed nation as well as on the other side of the world.

God asks that we be satisfied with our own circumstances, for being fulfilled wherever we happen to be helps us forget ourselves and our own difficulties, thereby enabling us to reach out to others in need. 'Give me neither poverty nor riches. Feed me with the food that is needful for me, lest I be full and deny thee and say "Who is the Lord?'' or lest I be poor and steal.'[6] Whether we have much or little we can be content if we walk with God; that way we neither deny Him nor fall into the temptation of thieving to make ends meet. Mind you, if injustice is clearly being done, then it is our duty to make a stand against such wrongdoing. In New Delhi, for example, zookeepers had to go on hunger strike to show their disquiet that the animals they looked after had almost twice as much money spent on their food each month as the keepers received in their monthly pay packet!

Do, however, be careful about how you respond to your friends and neighbours in need. When I was hard-up and on the dole, a number of well-meaning friends did offer to take me out for a meal. I was very grateful, but for me such generosity only worked once. Since I would have been quite happy to have been invited round to someone's house to share a cheap meal with them, I wondered at the apparent lack of sensitivity of those who took me out to a restaurant a number of times. It's certainly not nice to realize that you are being regarded as a charitable cause! Instead, visit someone in need with a gift of a cake you've made or such like, or ask them over for a snack; if they've been stuck at home unable to afford the fare to go anywhere else they'll enjoy the change of scene too.

There has always been poverty, and parents have always gone without food to feed their children when times are hard. We need to look out for such people in our midst. If there's someone in your class at school whose family are finding it difficult to make ends meet, occasionally invite them home for tea. If you use the school tuckshop regularly, share your bounty with those who don't have the spare cash to do so.

If you pass beggars in the street, don't just drop money into their hands – which could end up paying for alcohol or drugs – but give them some food or treat them to a cup of tea at a local caff instead. Money is faceless, whereas by handing over *food* you are interacting with someone in a much closer way; you begin to care about them.

Once on the London Underground system I came across a young man and his dog huddled on one of the stations with the now customary piece of battered cardboard informing commuters that both were hungry and homeless. I walked past feeling it too much of a hassle in the morning to rifle through my bag for some spare change. But on passing by I suddenly rememberd that I had an orange in my case. I stepped back and offered it. The following day the man and his dog were there again. I happened to have another orange in my bag. I handed it over and we both smiled – as if we'd shared a joke.

It's an idea to carry pieces of food around with you – an apple or carrot, a bar of chocolate to pep someone up on a cold, damp day – and make a point of looking out for people to share it with. A friend, Judy, who was a missionary in Pakistan tells me that she and her workmates never went out without a piece of fruit, because they knew beggars would come up to them wherever they happened to go. In this country there's been a lot of media attention on the number of con artists who rake in people's throwaway coins. Certainly there are people who do prey on those who give, but there are many genuine cases too. Young people who have been victims of abuse, thrown out of care or whose families can no longer afford to keep them, often end up on the city streets with no money or shelter. By giving people food you will be responding to genuine need; anybody who turns their nose up seems highly unlikely to be hungry and homeless.

Incidentally, if you regularly see young people begging it might be wise to find out the where-abouts of local shelters and refuges that you can direct them to if needs be. Then again, when I was a fairly new student in Manchester I was strolling through the city one evening when a tramp came up and asked the way to the Refuge Building. Not really engaging my brain, I duly pointed him in the direction of the grand Victorian building with its bright red lettering spelling 'Refuge' glowing from its tower for all Manchester to see; it was a local landmark, and only a few hundred yards down the road. It was only when I'd reached this point myself that I realized what I'd done. Not only was the building well and truly closed but I'd sent the poor man who was in search of refuge along to the Refuge *Assurance* offices. . . . I have this habit; once wandering around Kingston I came across a blind woman waiting at the kerb to cross the road. I did my civic duty and went up to her before passing along the street. 'It's OK, the little green man's there', I told her and walked on. A few yards down the street I realized what I'd done. I wondered if she had a clue what I was talking about. . . .

If you've got to know your local shopkeepers, ask them for any waste product they may have at the end of the week; restaurants, greengrocers and bakeries are particularly likely to have surplus they cannot use or sell, and supermarkets in exchange for some publicity may be prepared to help out too. Get your church or youth group to collect and distribute this food to those who must survive on low incomes in your local community.

In America, the Gleaning for the Hungry operation, which is part of the international body Youth With A Mission, collects less than perfect nectarines and peaches from Southern Californian fruit producers, processes and dries them under the hot American sun, and then distributes them to the poor as far afield as the Philippines and Cambodia. Rich in minerals and nutrients they are an important supplement to a basic rice diet. It is worthwhile that we consider how to redistribute waste food in our own localities.

In Europe, the Common Agricultural Policy deliberately ensures that Europe's own farmers are paid for their produce whether or not there is sufficient demand among Europe's people. This results in the obscenity of butter, wheat and barley mountains, and milk and wine lakes. While the European agricultural industry is protected by this policy Third World inhabitants not only die through lack of food, but because there is no room for their produce on the European market, and if it *is* bought it is at a price well below its real worth. World poverty is thus institutionalized, which for us as individuals can seem an insurmountable problem. Yet positive initiatives such as Gleaning for the Hungry, done in the name of Christ, are really redressing the balance.

Each one of us would be wise to consider how we can adjust our own lifestyles to help the hungry. If you're having a baking session, put aside some of your produce to distribute to another. Make use of doggy bags if you just can't manage that last slice of pizza when you're out for a meal in town, and hand it over to the next homeless person you meet. If you've been picking fruit or have an allotment, give away your surplus. Your actions might seem small gestures but each is one small step in the right direction. . . .

Action station

- Read:
  How to make the world less hungry by Kathy Keay (IVP 1990)
  Food for a future by Jon Wynne-Tyson (Thorsons 1977)
  Poverty and the planet by Ben Jackson/WDM (Penguin 1990)
  Beyond hunger by Art Beals (Kingsway 1987)
  Signs of our times by Charles Elliot (Marshall Pickering 1988)
  The developing world by Andrew Reed (Unwin Hyman 1987)

- 'Changemakers' is Christian Aid's youth network open to all young people who want to change the world for good. Write to Changemakers, Christian Aid, PO Box 100, London SE1 7RT for information on how to join.

- Choose to buy Oxfam, Tearcrfaft and Traidcraft products, which directly support Third World communities, in place of those sold by more exploitative food companies.

- Make a point of talking to those homeless people you meet on the street, and if you've the money, treating them to a cup of tea or a sandwich.

12
Fast Forward

Having got this far through a book called *Glorious Food*, a chapter about going without seems a bit out of place. Yet while we bring a Christian perspective to what we eat, God also adds a spiritual dimension to fasting and transforms the event. In the same way that, as we develop as Christians, our prayer life becomes a natural and everyday pursuit as easy as breathing, we also come to a point where we realize that just as eating can be a spiritual act, so too can the moments between.

Fasting – in its proper sense the act of going without food for God – cleans out the system on both a physical and spiritual level and makes us more receptive to God. By concentrating less on the physical side through our fast, we become less attached and in a sense restricted by our physical nature. 'The Christian who denies himself, becomes less important in his own eyes, and grows into an awareness of the glorious sovereignty of God.'[1]

But it's not enough just not to eat. Anybody can do that. For there are plenty of reasons not to, whether through dieting, or starving because there's not enough food to eat. We have to keep our mind on God.

The rhythm of our day is usually tied up with mealtimes. We get up, have breakfast (which incidentally is exactly what it says it is), at midday we eat lunch, we get home and have tea, and perhaps we'll also have supper later in the evening before we go to bed. As well as all the tea breaks and snacks we've had during the day. It's a habit. We do it every day. So by not eating, by breaking through that habit, we're going beyond the set-ups of ordinary life and day-to-day structure that we all tend to see as fundamental to living. We're actually breaking through that barrier. And that's very liberating. By fasting, our apparently empty day is now ready to be filled with activities that focus on our walk with God. The disciples didn't fast while Jesus was on earth, and the followers of John the Baptist couldn't understand the change in the Law: ' "How is it that we and the Pharisees fast, but your disciples do not fast?" Jesus answered, "How can the guests of the bridegroom mourn while he is with them? The time will come when the bridegroom will be taken from them; then they will fast." ' [2] With the resurrection after death, our fasting times are not of mourning, but rather of joy because of the hope we have in Jesus.

So it's important to use the time when we're not eating for God, to pray. For if we don't put God at the centre of the fasting experience, then it might as well just be an endurance test of how long we can go without food.

For it isn't the length of time that you fast that's

important, but the sincerity with which you do it. 'Our motive for fasting is much more important than the length of time we spend fasting.'[3] It's similar to praying. If you spend hours supposedly in prayer, but in fact your mind is wandering off down the alleys, unless you're determined to pull your thoughts back to God, your prayer time is being wasted and those wandering moments achieve nothing. In the same way, if we go without food but carry on with life as normal, without giving too much attention to God, what we're doing is not a fast, it's a crash diet.

Maybe there are friends of yours who need healing or do not know Christ. We can fast and pray for them to be made whole. Use the time to concentrate on that one person. If there's an issue in the news that deeply concerns you or a country you care about, make a day of praying about it.

There are times when we need to make major decisions in our lives, such as accepting a job offer, choosing a new church to go to, or a new home. In my own experience I've always tended to use the 'if the door opens' approach – the 'if God wants me here He'll allow me here' approach. Which certainly makes for much more relaxed interviews! Yet while it is a useful guide it is not necessarily the best. If you have a choice of more than one option then it doesn't work. One job I left after three months. Though it was 'a useful learning experience', as the saying goes, it perhaps wasn't the best job for me while I was doing it, even though it was the only job I'd been offered out of over a hundred applications. Instead of jumping in feet first out of sheer desperation (after all, there is a point when you've been turned down for so many jobs in your chosen field that you begin to feel that maybe you should go off and be a mastic asphalt spreader) it would have been better if on hearing that I'd been offered the job, I'd stood back from the situation and put the decision before God through prayer and fasting. It would have cleared things in my mind.

And it's those times when we're most unsure or unhappy and feel least like taking part in spiritual activities that it's best to partake; it can stop us from making foolhardy and time-wasting mistakes. It was through fasting and praying that the Church of Antioch heard God tell them to free Barnabus and Saul to do His work of mission,[4] and similarly the two men committed others to the Lord in the same way.[5] It was a key to strengthening the early Church and helping it to grow. In the same way we can get a clear sense of God's direction for our own life. And we won't be cushioned by our food, the comforter. We are alone with ourselves and God. It's the denying of our physicality, and there's no outside ingredient encroaching on the relationship.

From being a fairly neglected part of our Christian life, it is clear that we should seriously consider placing time aside on a regular basis to feed our spiritual life instead of our physical body. 'Almsgiving is one example of a duty which every believer has towards others, prayer is an example of a duty which he has towards God, and fasting is an example of one duty which he has towards himself.'[6]

Fit to fast

I once heard of a minister who lived in a particular Third World country where poverty and hardship were rife. On the days that he didn't have enough to eat he would declare, 'God would like me to fast today' and so would offer his hunger to God.

That's a noble response to a grim situation, but fasting should combine our own free will and our faith in God. For if someone we know is 'fasting' because they haven't enough food, then we should be asking ourselves what *we* are doing to feed them. And anyway, if you're starving or malnourished it's very difficult to concentrate your mind on higher things.

Some people regard fasting as an end in itself; they see it as a way of promoting health by clearing all the gunk out of their system. 'Fasting is nature's way of healing, but it is not a "cure-all" for every known ailment', explains Nicholas Saunders.[7] 'Total fasting makes it possible for nature to remove and expel foreign matter and disease-producing waste from the body. A traditional fasting drink is lemon juice mixed with honey', he concludes.

Technically this is not Christian fasting, but we can learn from it and adapt and take heed of it as part of our own fasting experience. All the grot comes to the surface within the first few days, so initially your skin looks awful and you won't feel too great either. But once the poisons have left your body you can feel thoroughly spring-cleaned. I'm sure you could get a sermon out of all that! For as Christians we can view this cleansing and expulsion process as a spiritual act too.

There are people who diet who assume that by going without food for a day they can lose a good bit of weight. But few realize that without being fuelled our body's metabolism slows down to compensate. You haven't the energy to do much and so you don't burn up any calories. One Ash Wednesday when I was a student, I decided that I'd offer the day to God by not eating. So I didn't eat. But I cycled to college, spent a day at lectures and in the library, and then cycled home absolutely shattered by five p.m. I felt so tired that I went straight to my bed to recover. I didn't know how to fast. I'd heard about fasting, but nobody had ever told me how one should go about it. My flatmates were stunned by my drained condition: 'Catherine, you're meant to take it easy, didn't you know?' Shortly afterwards when my flatmate's boyfriend fasted, he stayed at home and spent the day in a very low-key way listening to Christian tapes and reading.

The Jews are very aware of being in the right frame of mind for fasting. In general they seem to take the very idea of fasting more seriously than we Christians do. Eating is a very important part of their preparation for the fast they undertake annually on Yom Kippur, their Day of Atonement. They recognize that being too hungry tends to distract your mind from God. If you're physically weak and harsh hunger pangs make you think of what you'd like to eat, you're losing the point of the event.

But the previous day's eating is not simply a means of helping them withstand the rigours of fasting: 'Prayer is spiritual; eating is basic, instinctive. Judaism challenges man to elevate eating to the spiritual realm by considering it nourishment to enhance the service of God. On the day before Yom Kippur, we realize this ideal; by transforming ingestion and digestion into a preparation for the holy day.'[8]

The basic spiritual truth of regarding food as a means to help us work for God introduced in the Old Testament, is mirrored in the Christian gospels with an emphasis on appreciating it for its own sake as a gift of God. We add to the occasion by giving it back to Him.

When you choose to fast for God, it's not necessarily enough to go without food and focus your eyes on God. It's wise to take your health and what you're going to do that day into consideration too. 'If a Christian fasts, in a Christian way, he is not just disciplining his eating – he is symbolizing all of his personal life in one action. A Christian who fasts is, by virtue of his new nature in Christ, an abstainer in all respects; he does not carry anything to excess and always knows when to draw the line – as far as his bodily appetites are concerned.'[9]

As with dieting, if you're on any regular medication, then it's wise to consult your doctor first. I once planned to fast for Oxfam, but was advised by my own doctor to break the fast should I feel too weak. Interestingly enough, I found this to take a real weight off my mind. I could fast as long as I was able, I wasn't confined to any time limit, but to the limits of my own body.

Because denial, dying to self, is so much part of fasting it's very easy to fall into 'suffering' mode. There's a great temptation to let people know what you're putting yourself through. Jesus recognized this failing in us and warned against such show. 'When you fast, do not look sombre as the hypocrites do, for they disfigure their faces to show when they are fasting. I tell you the truth, they have received their reward in full. But when you fast, put oil on your head and wash your face, so that it will not be obvious to men that you are fasting, but only to your Father, who is unseen; and your Father, who sees what is done in secret, will reward you.'[10]

God spoke to me through this verse when I was on the dole, and revealed another way it could apply. It's very easy to fall into the 'life is tough' routine. When you haven't much money and you've got to make ends meet, the amount of food you eat goes down. And people you know tend to ask questions such as 'Is that all you're eating?' and it can be quite difficult to rise above the tone of such a question.

You go to sign on and stand in a stagnant queue in a grim, smoke-filled room full of people down on their luck, bawling babies, misery and frustration. It can easily get you down. But reading that verse about how you should behave when fasting, made me decide that I wasn't prepared to

look hard done by. I found some decent clothes at
the back of my wardrobe, even ironed them and
put some gunk on my face too. And held my head
up high.

It's the same sort of attitude that God wants us
to have when we give up our food for Him. The
only thing which should pass our lips, apart from
liquid, is a smile. But there *are* some people for
whom going without food is not just a trial but
potentially deadly. Derek Prince suggests that
Christians who are physically able to, fast also for
those such as diabetics for whom it could well
prove dangerous.[11] In my own situation I combine
the common sense of my doctor's advice with my
Christian duty. I give the situation to God, knowing that He knows that I can only give as much as
I can give, that I can only fast for as long as I can
fast.

Third World fast

Increasingly fasting is being adopted as a way of
raising money for projects in the Third World.
World Vision, a Christian Third World charity,
now has an annual twenty-four-hour fast designed
to raise money for emergency aid abroad. Partici-
pants include many young people, youth groups
and churches, schools and families. In 1991 the
fast's expected total of £2.5 million was to be
directed toward programmes in such places as
Ethiopia and Sudan.

I'm always a bit wary of the idea of sponsorship.
People talk about compassion fatigue, but there's

such a thing as sponsorship fatigue too. There's no problem the first time you do it, but friends can get fed up if you do too many sponsored events. But going round asking for money, perhaps knocking door-to-door, one can't help wondering why it's someone else that has to cough up the cash for *your* activity. And going without food for a set time to raise money for charity can for many people mean not a lot more than that, worthy though it may be. Whereas as Christians it is our responsibility to take the whole event very seriously. Think deeply about the people you're trying to help. Read up about the situation in developing countries and make sure you've got all the relevant packs and information from the organization for whom you're fasting. And learn the facts. Make the day a day of caring about people of the Third World, sharing with these people, while giving the day to Christ as well.

'Is not this the kind of fasting I have chosen: to loose the chains of injustice, and untie the cords of the yoke, to set the oppressed free and break every yoke? Is it not to share your food with the hungry and to provide the poor wanderer with shelter – when you see the naked, to clothe him and not to turn away from your own flesh and blood?'[12]

If you aren't really into sponsorship, consider instead simply saving money that you'd otherwise have spent on food and giving that away instead. CAFOD has a twice yearly 'Family fast day' where supporters are encouraged to give up a meal or some luxury and send the money saved to finance the feeding, clothing, housing and educating of the poor of the Third World.

Forced fast

Sometimes due to circumstances beyond our control, we must go without food. While working our way through the situation we can also offer it up to God. So if you can't afford a meal, you should not only pray that God will provide, but be positive too in those moments while you're waiting.

A recent experience of having to live 'nil by mouth' was when I had my wisdom teeth out under general anaesthetic. The whole experience became a very special day of being close to God. It's been said that fasting reveals the side of us that is cushioned by food. So in the same way that perhaps past angers and hurts rise to the surface, as Christians God uses the time to heighten our spiritual awareness.

Admittedly I found myself going out for a binge the night before I went into hospital; a real case of 'Well, if I'm not going to eat at all tomorrow, I might as well pig out tonight'. But though I jokingly remarked to a fellow patient that it had been like one's last meal before execution, I knew it was nothing compared to the case of an American criminal who'd met Jesus on Death Row, which crossed my mind. While most people's last supper tends to be a bit of a stodge out – a steak and chips for instance – this Christian had calmly requested unleavened bread and a glass of wine, and used the night before his death to pray and prepare himself. In the light of his Christian faith he accepted the consequences for his past and treated the whole thing in a very sacramental way.

In my own situation, even though I was forced to fast, God still used the occasion as if I'd fasted of my own accord. On my way to Guy's Hospital to have the op, as I clambered up the steps leading from London Bridge tube station, I noticed a young woman begging on the down side of the steps. It suddenly occurred to me that as I wasn't eating that day, I had money to spend on food. It was no skin off my nose to go and buy a filled roll and a cup of tea and offer it to her. I always feel in such situations that I *should* say something about my Christian faith and why I'm helping the person out, but I'm afraid I find it very difficult to do. But as I handed over the food I said a quick 'God bless you', and as I turned and trotted back up the steps and on to the street, I felt a great wave of sorrow washing over me and I wanted to weep for her. I'd gone down to the girl very calm and collected. I'd come away with God breaking through my cool exterior.

The operation itself gave me nothing to worry about and nor did God. In that twilight post-op world between clear consciousness and deep sleep, I found my head full of praise songs, which for me was rather ironic. When I'm wide awake I can be quite scathing about the lack of brain cells needed to sing a lot of the modern songs. Yet when you're half anaesthetized without the strength to grip onto consciousness, they're ideal! I found myself mentally humming and chatting

away to God within the twilight zone. With no
food around I had literally to eat my words!

If you're living with your parents or are a lodger
it can be difficult to fast for a whole day. People,
particularly if they aren't Christians, can get a bit
concerned if they know someone's missing meals.
God knows our situation, and so we can tell him:
'Look God, I'm in this position. I would like to fast
for longer but I can't.' And it makes you realize
that giving up small things, given to God in all
faith, can be just as important and effective.
Instead of full fasting, go without supper, that
snack at break time or the second helping that
you'd normally have. You could miss your school
dinner occasionally, though don't get into this on
too regular a basis, for as a growing adolescent,
you'll very likely need the energy from *all* of your
meals. Or try walking past that sweet shop you
originally planned to pop into on your way home
from school or work. And give away the money
you save, either to organizations that support
people in the Third World, such as Oxfam, Tear
Fund or CAFOD, or give it away to someone in
need, whether that's a close friend who's short of
cash, or the person begging whom you happen to
be passing in the street.

It's about denying ourself and giving the
moment to God. It's so easy to be greedy, and in
saying 'no' we are making a definite '*self*-denial'.
We're stopping ourselves short of eating and realizing that we can get by without food for a certain
amount of time. It helps us to realize that food
doesn't have as much hold on us as we tend to

believe. By letting go of our bodily needs just for a while, we're giving our whole attention to God.

Action station

- Read:
    How to fast successfully by Derek Prince (Cassette Books 1976)
    Fasting: a neglected discipline by David Rushworth Smith (New Wine Press 1989)
    God's chosen fast: a spiritual and practical guide by Arthur Wallis (Victory Press 1968)

- Start small and build up your length of fast gradually. To start with, go without supper. The next time miss lunch so that you're fasting from breakfast to breakfast. Extend your fast by a meal each time you do it, to your personal limit.

- For details regarding fasting to support programmes in the Third World, call World Vision on 0604 32324 or write to CAFOD, PO Box 777, London SW9 9TZ.

- It can be difficult if you live in a non-Christian household where meals are prepared for you. But if you're about to reach out for a slice of cake, instead hold back and offer that 'doing without' to God, the same with snacks. Cut down on what you eat between meals.

Notes

1. Introduction

1. Matthew 4:4.
2. Geoffrey Cannon, *The Politics of Food*, Century 1987, p. 16.
3. Anne Arnott, *Fruits of the Earth*, Mowbray 1979.
4. 1 Corinthians 6:19.
5. Derek Prince, *How to Fast Successfully*, Cassette Books 1976, p. 19.
6. Genesis 3:6–7.
7. Tony Campolo, *The Kingdom of God is a Party*, Word 1990, p. 93.
8. Matthew 4:19.
9. Matthew 13:47–48.

2. Mirror, Mirror on the Wall

1. Michel Tournier, *The Midnight Love Feast*, Collins 1991, p. 8.
2. Genesis 1:31.
3. Genesis 3:7.
4. Ann Edwards, This is the thin end of the wedge. Letter to the *Daily Mail*, 15th February 1991.
5. Chrissie Iley, 'Don't call me cosy!', The *Daily Mail*, 22nd July 1991, p. 7.

6. Andrea James, 'Love, sex, and the dieting woman', *New Woman*, June 1991, p. 12.
7. Rosemary Conley, *Rosemary Conley's Hip and Thigh Diet*, Arrow 1989, p. 23.

3. Celebrate the Feast
1. Luke 22:17–19.
2. Deuteronomy 14:22–27.
3. Luke 15:3–7.
4. Matthew 18:20.
5. Catherine Swift, *Catherine Bramwell-Booth*, Heroes of the Cross series, Marshall Pickering 1989, p. 69.

4. Eating Out
1. Mark 8:2, 6–8.
2. Mark 2:15–17.
3. Matthew 11:18–19.

5. Store Checkout
1. Matthew 6:25–27.
2. Jonathon Holliman, *A Consumer's Guide to the Protection of the Environment*, Pan/Ballantine 1971, p. 48.
3. Leigh Reinhold, 'Cornered by shopping', Mirror Woman, The *Daily Mirror*, 12th June 1991, pp. 6–7.
4. Amanda Byron-Jones, IFE 91 – An overview, *Press information published at IFE 91*, 28th April 1991.
5. Tesco Advice Centre, *A Tesco Guide to Healthy Eating*, Tesco Advice Centre, Hertfordshire.
6. *How do Britain's top companies rate in areas of social and environmental responsibility?* promotion

leaflet for *Changing corporate values* by Richard Adams et al., New Consumer 1991.

7. Janet Hunt, *A Vegetarian in the Family*, Thorsons 1977.
8. Genesis 2:3.

6. From the Freezer to the Microwave

1. Nigel Slater, 'Time to give the chill cabinet the cold shoulder', The *Sunday Correspondent*, 4th March 1990.
2. Matthew 13:33.
3. Department of the Environment, *Wake up to what you can do for the environment* pamphlet, Department of the Environment 1991.
4. Dr Richard Lacey, *Safe Shopping, Safe Cooking, Safe Eating*, Penguin 1989, p. 149.

7. Growing Your Own

1. Genesis 2:15.
2. Genesis 3:17–19.
3. Matthew 12:1–2.
4. Mervyn Wilson, *The Rural Spirit*, Harper Collins 1990, p. 83.
5. John 15:1–2.
6. Matthew 13:3–8.
7. Proverbs 3:9–10.

8. Too Many Cooks

1. Jonathon Porritt, ed. *Friends of the Earth Handbook*, MacDonald Optima 1987, p. 56.
2. Jonathon Holliman, *Consumers Guide to the Protection of the Environment*, Pan/Ballantine 1971, p. 48.
3. Leslie Kenton, Foreword to first edition *in*

Maurice Hanssen, *E for Additives*, Thorsons 1988, p. 9.

4. Jonathon Porritt, ed. *as above*, p. 51–52.
5. Maurice Hanssen, *E for Additives*, Thorsons 1988.
6. John Biggs, 'The ethics of patenting life itself', *Baptist Times*, 13th June 1991.
7. Deborah Gaskell, Protecting food crops from pests, Hi-Chem: special advertising section, *Time*, 15th January 1990.
8. Joan and Derek Taylor, eds, *Safe Food Handbook*, Ebury 1990, p. 63.
9. Sir Julian Rose, 'Irradiation as health hazard', *The Times*, 20th January 1990.
10. 'New concern over patenting of life', *The War Cry*, 25th May 1991, p. 2.

9. Eat Your Greens

1. Matthew 15:17–18.
2. Genesis 1:29–30.
3. Genesis 9:1–3.
4. Matthew 10:29.
5. Romans 14:3.
6. Romans 14:1–2.
7. Romans 14:6.
8. Leaflet on vegetarianism, Christian Ecology Link.
9. Doris Longacre, *More With Less Cookbook*, Lion 1987, p. 150.
10. Genesis 9:4.
11. Daniel 1:8–20.

10. Factory Flaw

1. Jonathon Porritt, ed. *Friends of the Earth Handbook*, Macdonald Optima 1987, p. 60.

2. Genesis 1:26.
3. Matthew 18:12–13.
4. Vegan Society, *Slaughter of the Innocent*, leaflet, p. 2.
5. Andrew Linzey, *Christianity and the Rights of Animals*, SPCK 1987, p. 112.
6. Sarah Stancliffe, 'A vegetarian in the family', The *Church Times*, 15th February 1991.
7. John Webster, 'Sense and sensibility down on the farm', The *New Scientist*, 21st July 1988, pp. 41–44.
8. Andrew Linzey, *as above*, p. 114.
9. Maurice Hanssen, *E for Additives*, Thorsons 1988, p. 35.
10. Andrew Linzey, *as above*, p. 15.

11. The Starving Hungry

1. James 2:15–17.
2. Jonathon Porritt, ed. *Friends of the Earth Handbook*, Macdonald Optima 1987, p. 51.
3. Kathy Keay, *How to make the world less hungry*, IVP Frameworks 1990, p. 12.
4. Kathy Keay, *as above*, p. 21.
5. Vegetarian Society, *Before you eat Meat, Digest this Leaflet* pamphlet, p. 3.

12. Fast Forward

1. David Rushworth Smith, *Fasting: A Neglected Discipline*, New Wine Press 1988.
2. Matthew 9:14–15.
3. Derek Prince, *How to Fast Successfully*, Cassette Books 1976, p. 57.
4. Acts 13:1–3.
5. Acts 14:23.
6. David Rushworth Smith, *as above*, p. 10.

7. Nicholas Saunders, *Alternative London* 3
   Nicholas Saunders 1972, p. 51.
8. Yossi Prager, Rosh Hashana and Yom Kippur
   in Naomi Black ed. *Celebration: the book of
   Jewish Festivals*, Collins 1987, p. 17.
9. David Rushworth Smith, *as above*, p. 17.
10. Matthew 6:18.
11. Derek Price, *as above*, p. 17.
12. Isaiah 58:6